The Question is the Answer

Focusing on Solutions with Cognitive Hypnotherapy

About the author

Trevor Silvester was a police officer for eighteen years before leaving to become a hypnotherapist and trainer. With his wife Rebecca he launched the Quest Institute in 2000, the first school in the world training people to be Cognitive Hypnotherapists – the approach he developed. It is now the largest organisation of its type.

He was editor of the *Hypnotherapy Journal* for nine years, and is currently the Director of Supervision and Ethics for the National Council for Hypnotherapy. In 2007 he was awarded the Hartland Prize for his contribution to hypnotherapy.

In addition to running training courses and writing he also has a private practice in Harley Street.

To my Mum and Dad with love

The Question is the Answer

Focusing on Solutions with Cognitive Hypnotherapy

Trevor Silvester

Foreword by Gil Boyne

THE QUEST INSTITUTE

Text copyright © Trevor Silvester 2006
First published by The Quest Institute 2006
Old Ness Farm, Ness Road, Burwell, Cambs, CB5 0DB
website questinstitute.co.uk
Second Edition 2011

The author can be contacted on email
Trevor@questinstitute.co.uk
www.questinstitute.co.uk

The moral right of Trevor Silvester to be identified as the author of this work has been asserted in accordance with the Copyright, Designs and Patents Act 1988

All rights reserved. This book is sold subject to the condition that it shall not, by way of trade or otherwise, be lent, resold, hired out or otherwise circulated without the publisher's prior consent in any form of binding or cover other than that in which it is published and without a similar condition including this condition being imposed on the subsequent purchaser.

British Library Cataloguing in Publication Data
A catalogue record for this book is available from the British Library

ISBN 978-0-9543664-2-1

Typeset by Amolibros, Milverton, Somerset
This book production has been managed by Amolibros
Printed and bound by T J International Ltd, Padstow, Cornwall, UK

Contents

Foreword	ix
Acknowledgements	xi
Introduction	1

Part I: Gaining direction   9

1 Making a start   10
    Identifying the problem state   13
    Pattern hunting   13
    Context   17
    Structure   24
    Process   29
    The Solution state: begin with the end in mind   34
    Defining their outcome   35
    Future pacing using Neuro Logical Levels   37

2 Questions are the answer   46

3 The Boynian pattern   60
    Identifying their evidence for the problem state   64
    Identifying their evidence for the solution state   71

4 Listening for trance   78

5   The importance of the last ten minutes   85

Part II: Creating and delivering the suggestion 93

6   Creating the suggestion   94
    Session two: delivering the suggestion   101

Part III: Gauging the differences that make the difference 103

7   Calibrating and using change   104
    Change-link pattern   106

Part IV: The last piece of the jigsaw 111

8   The importance of consequence   112
    Consequence   112
    The Rocking-Chair exercise   120

9   Think yourself lucky   123
    Conclusion   150

Appendices 165

Appendix 1	The therapeutic paradox	166
Appendix 2	NLLs	172
Appendix 3	The meta-model	175
Appendix 4	Meta-model questions	178
Appendix 5	Reframing	186
Appendix 6	Suggestion starters	191

Glossary   193
Bibliography   207
Notes   209
Index   211

Foreword

Trevor will tell you later that we met following his attending a masterclass of mine. As the editor of the *Hypnotherapy Journal* in England he arranged to interview me and duly arrived at my home with his tape recorder. And so began a friendship.

His interview heralded a collaboration that had the initial purpose of creating my biography, but instead became a pleasant eighteen months of chats, and lunches. At least so I thought. Now seeing the emergence of the Boynian pattern as an offspring of our enjoyable meetings I realise the good use he made of our time.

In many ways ours is an unlikely friendship. Not only are we separated by age, but by approach. As someone who's always shied from models and theories I've seen Neuro-Linguistic Programming (NLP) grow into an influential force in therapy, without ever becoming personally attracted to the study of it. I believe therapy involves the transformation of negative affect and getting the client to get in touch with the inner part that is divine. Trevor's approach is far more scientific and much less spiritual, which I guess is the way the world is going.

I suspect some people might find it strange that I am writing the foreword to a book that integrates theories and models from a wide range of fields. I hope at my age I'm wise enough to realise that none of us has a monopoly on what's right. What is evident throughout this book is the breadth and depth of the author's knowledge and the ability he has to bring ideas from different fields together in a coherent and compelling way, and I'm pleased that some of those ideas are mine!

I remember telling Trevor over one of our lunches that I saw in him one of the future leaders of our profession. As an activist I take pride in what I've achieved in promoting the benefits of hypnotherapy and developing it as a profession, now it's time for a new generation to continue the work. Within this book, for all the differences between Trevor's philosophy and mine, I see Trevor's passion, intelligence and desire to advance that many will respond to, which gives me confidence that his intention is the same as mine – to free people from their limitations and help them live blessed lives.

I'm proud to have been an influence on Trevor, but you can see clearly within this writing that I am only one of several. We're all standing on the shoulders of giants. I'm standing on the shoulders of Fritz Perls and Dave Elman, and now my shoulders share Trevor's weight. I have no doubt that in time his shoulders will be ones that others seek to climb upon.

I commend this book to you, understanding its concepts can only help to make you a better therapist.

With respect to all, Gil Boyne

Acknowledgements

Where do I start? I've been blessed with so many wonderful influences along the way that I'm in danger of turning this into a Gwyneth Paltrow acceptance speech. Prompted by Martin Seligman's ideas on gratitude I'd like to start with the many teachers of English who inspired in me a love of reading and words. Among them; Mrs Hopkins, Elizabeth Summers, Mr Barron and Mr Godwin. Like most good teachers I suspect this acknowledgement of their influence is long overdue.

It's appropriate that I mention again Gil Boyne. Since his move back to the USA our contact has been more intermittent, but I've felt his influence keenly as I've written this book. I hope it adds to his deserved legacy.

I can add to the list of people who've been an influence but who I've yet to meet, Martin Seligman, whose wonderful book *Authentic Happiness* has been a profound influence, as well as Professor Richard Wiseman. The area of Positive Psychology continues to inspire.

At the 2005 National Council for Hypnotherapy conference I listened to Rubin Battino speak again and was privileged to share some time with him. A rare man whose spirit with his clients is something I aspire to, as is the lightness and openness of Dr Brian Roet.

I have been truly lucky to have made so many friends from those who began as students. The quality of people attracted to The Quest Institute gives me confidence that we're doing things right and that a healthy future awaits Cognitive Hypnotherapy. I'd like them all to consider themselves individually thanked for what they've taught me, and the fun I've had teaching them. Two who deserve special mention are Isobel Scott and Sue Knight who were test readers of the book as it evolved; it was a wonderful thing to witness the book I had in my head emerge from the original manuscript as they skilfully hacked and slashed at it.

Isobel is a wonderfully talented hypnotherapist who has been a big part of The Quest Institute since its beginning, and has been a good friend even longer. Her grasp of grammar probably made my writing quite painful for her, but her eye for detail helped my ideas flow much more coherently.

Sue's background is typical of the spirit we seem to attract to our courses. Sue was a successful criminal defence lawyer, but in her forties decided that slaving away for seventy hours a week simply couldn't compete with travelling around the world. After a couple of years teaching, she eventually settled in Mallorca, where, as her free bus pass looms, she now enjoys a third career as a Barefoot Therapist, when not writing, drawing cartoons or ruthlessly improving my writing. As a former police officer I never expected to find a lawyer with integrity, let alone one I respect and love so much. It's been a rewarding surprise.

And finally, above all, my wife Rebecca, whose patience with me is immense, and whose belief in me seems even greater. She is more important to me than she can ever know.

I know I said finally, but he'll sulk if I don't mention him this time; our Yorkie, Barney. He has a heart bigger than his head and never lets us forget what's truly important. Him

Introduction

Life would be so much easier if you knew how things were going to develop before you began them, wouldn't it?

When I first published *Wordweaving: The Science of Suggestion* in 2003 I had been teaching a course based on my ideas about therapy for about three years. I had called the approach Cognitive Hypnotherapy to distinguish it from the traditional ideas of trance and suggestion, and to emphasise the importance of the individual client's cognitions in the formation of both their problem and solution.

That book introduced a key part of my teaching – a model of hypnotic language that is geared towards using the client's own imagination in creating perceptions that free them from their limitations, and its impact has been such that it regularly still appears at the top of the British Amazon hypnotherapy sales chart eight years later. Perhaps I tapped into a collective feeling that one-size-fits-all suggestions just couldn't be the most effective way of influencing an individual mind, or maybe it's just a cool title.

This book followed in 2006 as the next step in exploring the features of Cognitive Hypnotherapy, by describing a way of working that integrates the use of such tailored suggestion into a therapy framework that guides you from the first session to the last. I decided that a change of title was necessary to reflect that Wordweaving™ exists within this rich therapeutic framework, rather than as something separate.

Changing the name of a book that has been available for five years isn't a step to be taken lightly, but I feel that its title now properly reflects its place within the three book series that my 2010 publication, *Cognitive Hypnotherapy: What's that about and How can I use it?*, completed. Taken together they form a comprehensive approach for helping people change, I just wish I could have known them all in their complete forms before I began any of them – at the very least it would have prevented the need for the name change – but I guess that's the way things evolve. I could have had no idea in 2003 how far Cognitive Hypnotherapy would come in offering a new way of thinking about therapy.

This book is written on the assumption that you've read *Wordweaving*. What I want to achieve here is:

> To assist you in obtaining from the client the information you need to create a suggestion pattern that derives from their model of the world, with the minimum of contamination from your own.

> To develop a series of steps that guide you in the development of your suggestions, and your choice of intervention, as your therapy progresses with a client.

> To show you how to re-tune the client's unconscious to motivate them to change and to anticipate and notice evidence that supports their improvement.

The three steps of Wordweaving™ still apply:

1. Identify what aspect of the client's experience your suggestion is aimed at changing.
2. Choose which mental processes, usually termed 'trance phenomena' should be used to achieve that shift in perception in your client.
3. Linguistically frame the suggestion to achieve that aim.

Now we are concerned with going deeper into how you identify the client's experience, what trance phenomena provide the most leverage in assisting them to change, and providing you with a model of therapy you can follow that fits it all together into a session - and then how to adjust your suggestions to reflect the changes they achieve as therapy progresses. What I've been very aware of as I've written this book is the need to pretend that therapy is a linear process where you smoothly progress from Plan A to Plan B. In reality we know that therapy involves false starts, blind alleys, setbacks, various diversions – some of them necessary – and overlap. If I'd attempted to explain a model to you that incorporated these real-time twists and turns I think my limitations as a writer would have left us all confused, so I've sacrificed some reality for (I hope) the sake of clarity. Please bear this in mind.

We're often asked, "How many sessions will I need?" That's always a difficult thing to answer. The public's perception has been shifted away from the Freudian expectation of therapy taking years, to one that expects change quickly. And, generally, that's a good thing because of course rapid change is perfectly possible, but it depends on the client, their problem, the quality of your relationship with them, and your ability to choose the right approach. It also depends on the flow of the therapy from session-to-session, one of the hardest things for new therapists – and even experienced ones – to gauge. How do you keep track of where you are, and when you're done? It is so easy to get lost in the sometimes meandering unravelling of a client's problem.

An excellent graduate of ours, Jane Hodgkin, helped me to clarify how to explain how to pace this, and gave me the inspiration for the framework presented in this book. She realised, in her early months of practice, that she fretted over this question "how long?" She even realised that she prompted the end of therapy before its outcome had been consolidated because she feared she wasn't giving the client value. Like so many therapists she hadn't yet learnt to use the client's outcome to calibrate the progress of the therapy. Then she had the simple insight that solved her problem. She turned her therapy into a series of programmes. Jane specialises in pain-free birth, so with this it's particularly easy to explain the principle. There was a certain number of things she wanted to achieve to ensure the client got what she wanted, and the therapy takes the time it takes until that number of things are achieved. Some clients tick the box quicker than others. So the response to "how long?" becomes, "There are a number of things we need to achieve for you to get to where you want to go. We'll know as you reach each step so we will always be able to gauge that you're making progress. Different people progress at different speeds so it might take four sessions, and it might take more. How quickly isn't as important to me as how permanently." I'm all for quick fixes, but only those that stick.

This book evolved from my realisation that my training hadn't provided enough structure about the progress of therapy, prompted by Jane's insight. When using suggestions in hypnosis there is no set way of knowing how quickly the client will respond to them. I do not believe in the mythical 'perfect' script for smoking/weightloss/confidence etc. We are all unique so how can there be a 'one-size-fits-all solution?'

INTRODUCTION

Words delivered in a session one week may sometimes need to be adapted in the next session in response to the changes they've created in the client, although if you have phrased your use of their language at a high enough level of vagueness you'll find that their unconscious continues to adapt your phrases to fit the continuing movement towards improvement.

So there will be occasions where delivering just one suggestion pattern once will be enough to resolve their issue, but it's also wise to have a framework for you to follow for those occasions where it isn't.

The steps are shown overleaf (NB all the terms within the framework will be explained as the book progresses):

Sometimes you will gain the initial information in a single session of one hour. Sometimes you will have everything you need in just 20 minutes, occasionally it might take several sessions. However long this first step takes, it is the key to your success. You must have a clear idea of what to say before you use an intervention or suggestion. You'll notice sessions 3 + and 4 +. The + is intended to indicate that really each of these sessions might extend over several appointments, and that elements of step 4 might be initiated while in the latter stages of step 3. As I've said already, therapy is not something that fits neatly into a paint-by-numbers box, so these latter steps illustrate principles to follow according to the progress of the client, rather than being carved in stone as to when they should be introduced. This book is going to follow that four step sequence using a theoretical client called Helen. We will follow the course of her therapy, taking time-outs to explain the ideas that underpin what I'm suggesting. Where the time-outs would have interrupted the flow of ideas too much I've included them as appendices instead. In my third book we meet Helen again as we use the information extracted here to guide us through choices of interventions and techniques.

As is so often the case, a story provides the most eloquent means of explaining what this book is about:

DIRECTION
Session One:

- Identify client's problem state, using context, structure and process questions.

- Identify client's solution state by defining their outcome and using the Neuro-logical level future pace.

DELIVERY
Session Two:

- Choose a technique to reframe the Context of their problem or change its Structure or interrupt its Process (or a combination of these).

- Use the information from session one to create a suggestion pattern that gets them to notice their problem state less and anticipate their desired state more.

CALIBRATION
Session Three+:

- Calibrate whether the client perceives themselves to be improving.

- If they do, use the Change-Link Pattern. Consider further interventions if appropriate.

- If they don't then adjust the aim of your suggestions and continue using techniques to change the problem pattern. Continue until success is achieved.

CONSEQUENCE
Session Four+:

- Once client is experiencing positive change include visualisations to prime the mind for positive expectancy (Rocking Chair and Luck Scripts).

- End therapy when client considers themselves to have achieved their goal(s) and progress appears ongoing and self-sustaining.

Developers build the world's most advanced office building. It's the biggest in the world and is crammed with high-tech gizmos. However, disaster strikes on the day it's opened; the button is pressed to fire up the state-of-the-art air-conditioning system – and nothing happens! Without it the building can't be occupied, so they make no money. Financial ruin rears its ugly head. The original suppliers can't figure out what's wrong and a long procession of experts and consultants all end up shaking their heads and walking away – usually just after charging the developers thousands for not being able to help. Finally they're reduced to going through Yellow Pages, and the last person on the list is one of those free lineage ads:

For all Plumbing and Heating problems call me.

With nowhere left to go an appointment is made and in due course this old guy turns up in overalls that look even older than he is, clutching a bag of tools. Taking care not to brush against him in their designer suits the developers lead him down into the bowels of the building to the big room where all the plumbing stuff lives. The old guy walks away from them to the centre of the room and just stands there, listening...and listening. The developers try listening as well, but can't hear anything and begin to grow bored. Then, suddenly, the old guy leans down to his bag and picks from it a small hammer. He walks over to an innocuous looking valve on the wall, seemingly identical to dozens of others, and taps on it once, firmly. The effect is amazing. Instantly the whole building comes alive, with the air con gurgling and wheezing away happily. One of the developers – forgetting her suit – shakes his hand warmly, "Thank you so much, you're a genius." With similar exaltations ringing in his ears he quietly leaves.

A couple of weeks later the finance director opens the mail and finds inside an envelope a tatty piece of paper. It's the invoice from the plumber. In pencil is written, 'for service rendered, £30,000'. The finance director hits the roof. "He wasn't here more than fifteen minutes, how can he charge that much?!" He rattles off a query,

> Dear Sir,
>
> In respect of your recent invoice please can you provide us with an itemised breakdown of your bill.
>
> Yours etc...

Another fortnight goes by and a second piece of tatty paper arrives on the finance director's desk. It's from the plumber:

> Dear Sir,
>
> In respect of your query here is the breakdown of the services I provided to you;
> For use of the hammer, £5.
> For knowing where to tap.............£29995.

Most of all, this book is about learning where to tap.

Part I

Gaining direction

> **DIRECTION Session One:**
>
> - Identify client's problem state, using context, structure and process questions.
>
> - Identify client's solution state by defining their outcome and using the Neuro-logical level future pace.

Chapter 1

Making a start

Helen's my eleven a.m. It's her first time and I'm not sure what she wants me to help her with, just some vague, nervous generalities on the phone about feeling stuck. She rang me on recommendation from another client and I generally vet referrals less before we meet. She walks in and sits in my therapy chair, but doesn't make use of its comfort; she sits forward, almost as if she's ready to charge back out of the door. I make a bit of small talk to settle her (and me) down. The atmosphere is charged with anticipation, nervousness and hope. Where do I go from here? Isn't that what we all wonder? There is infinite possibility in the direction that therapy can take, and if therapy were a dance it would be a tango – because it takes two. There is no way that we, as the therapists, can avoid influencing the way it develops. Let me pause Helen as I explain. We'll return to her a little later (or a lot later if you read slowly).

Because of the subjectivity of the problem we, as therapists, influence and shape the client's perception of the problem from the beginning of the interview process. In the words of Bill Hudson O'Hanlon and Michelle Weiner-Davis,

> What we choose to focus upon, what we choose to ignore, the way in which we word our questions, whether we decide to interrupt or

remain silent – all help shape the picture of the client's situation.[1]

All of the above will derive from the beliefs we hold about what it takes for someone to be helped, and what information we collect will be based on what we think is important about a client's problem. So the theoretical model we apply to the problem will help to define it for the client. A client with a psychoanalyst is likely to begin to view the problem in terms of an unresolved Oedipus complex; with a Jungian therapist it might be an imbalance between anima and animus (male and female elements of the personality), and with a Behaviourist it will be the observable behaviour that will become the focus of their attention.

I am no different. As a Cognitive Hypnotherapist I am guided equally by my beliefs. One that will guide the way this book evolves is this:

> Clients have all the resources they need to solve their problem; it is the function of the therapist to utilise the clients' potential, not to provide the answer.

I hear many therapists claiming to work in this way – in what can be called the Ericksonian tradition, and yet our beliefs are so pervasive that they intrude very easily into the way we couch questions and suggestions. As this book progresses I will continually remind you to ask the question that gets the clients to solve their problem, not try to come up with the solution yourself, because their idea is almost inevitably a better fit in their model of the world than yours can hope to be.

Wordweaving™ forms part of the therapeutic approach I call Cognitive Hypnotherapy that is both problem and solution focused; problem focused in that recoding the roots of limiting beliefs and negative emotions by the use of regression and other techniques offers a powerful means of rapid change, and solution focused in that it seeks to adjust both the present perceptions of our clients, and the way they begin to anticipate the future. The main thrust of this volume is aimed at the solution end of therapy, so in the main the information-gathering questions I suggest you pose to your clients are for the purpose of identifying what perceptions need changing, and how their imagining of the future can be adjusted.

So, going back to the question posed with me sitting in front of my new client, 'Where do I go from here?' Consider this question:

> *What do I need to know, which by knowing it provides the means to resolve the problem?*

What I suggest we need to know is:

A What is preventing them from having what they want? I call this the *problem state*.
B What is their outcome from therapy – i.e. what do they want that they don't currently have? I call this the *solution state*.

The essence of this approach is to establish as clearly as possible everything that makes up the pattern of the clients' issue – their problem state – and then identify their evidence for being without their problem – their solution state; what do they want versus what do they have? Once we've established these two ends of the continuum our job is to get them out of the problem state and as far along the road to their solution state as it's possible to get them.

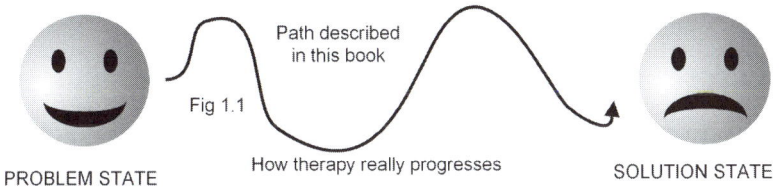

PROBLEM STATE — Fig 1.1 — Path described in this book — How therapy really progresses — SOLUTION STATE

Identifying the problem state

One of the most common problems for the therapist is therapist fatigue. Often without realising it the therapist gets involved in the emotions of the story and starts to share the clients' feelings. It's easily done, we hear terrible stories and our bodies respond to them as if they're our own. Over time our immune system gets exhausted and we end up feeling worse than some of our clients. It's the fast track to burnout. If you take on the feelings of the client it will exhaust you and make you miserable – at best. In Cognitive Hypnotherapy we train the therapist to listen for specific categories of information. This goes a long way to avoiding getting lost or involved in the content. The four categories of information are **structure, process, context** and **consequence.** Your questions should be mainly aimed at obtaining information about these categories, because they make up the *problem state* that is the clients' perception of their issue.

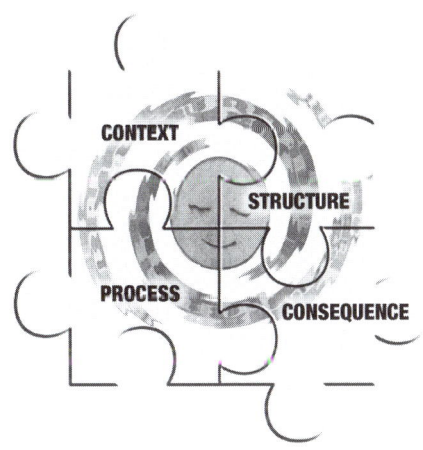

Pattern hunting

My grandfather introduced me, as a boy, to chess. I was immediately enthralled. Long evenings were spent huddled over the board, both of us taking a childlike glee in the tussle for victory. Memories I will always treasure. In my efforts to improve I read books on tactics, studied famous matches between grandmasters and joined the school club, hooked on the infinite variety of patterns that emerge from such a limited range of moves with so few pieces. Until recently I had no inkling of how chess provides a metaphor for a great deal of what our brain concerns itself with. As the Futurist Ray Kurzweil writes,

> Humans are far more skilled at recognizing patterns than in thinking through logical combinations, so we rely on this aptitude for almost all of our mental processes. Indeed, pattern recognition comprises the bulk of our neural circuitry. These faculties make up for the extremely slow speed of human neurons.[2]

Strange to think of the brain as being slow, but he means slow if made to work in a particular way – that is, not the way evolution has shaped it. The human brain is made up of neurons that struggle with problems that need to be solved serially – one calculation after another. Neurons require a 'reset time' of about five milliseconds, meaning that neurons are capable of only 200 calculations per second compared to the PC I'm writing this on, which can do millions of calculations per second. It's why we let them do the heavy lifting for anything that requires repetitive maths skills. It also shows a limit to the computer analogy that cognitive theory is based on – the brain is a computer – but it's evolved to solve particular problems. Our ancestors' brains had to recognise patterns that equalled shelter, food, sex and danger far more often than they had to work out the square root of 490 (answers on a postcard). Unlike our serial PCs, the brain is a massively parallel system, with 100 billion neurons all working away at the same time. That parallelism allows the brain to perform amazing feats of pattern recognition;

feats that continue to confound digital computers – such as remembering faces. The early enthusiasm of artificial intelligence has been tempered by the realisation that tasks we take for granted – like face recognition – are within the scope of a six-month-old child, but beyond the ability of a computer that can calculate the trajectory of a satellite sent to intercept a comet millions of miles away. A computer program designed to play chess works serially through the different move options, so its level of difficulty is based on how much time you give it to make its calculations.

I remember the earliest model I ever bought used to take minutes to come up with its move, but the increase in processing power now makes the computer's time delay between novice and master levels almost unnoticeable, though it's still doing it the same way. Humans play chess differently. Their brain doesn't look at every piece one at a time and work out all possibilities that could arise from moving it. As Granddad and I peered down at the board our minds were hard at work detecting patterns in the game, predicting consequences, seeing areas of strength and weakness – and our ability to recognise these patterns improves with experience.

Because each individual neuron is so slow, Kurzweil explains,

> ...we don't have time...to think too many new thoughts when we are pressed to make a decision. The human brain relies on pre-computing its analyses and storing them for reference. We then use our pattern recognition capability to recognise a situation as compatible to one we have thought about and then draw upon our previously considered conclusions.[3]

So in our early encounters Granddad beat me easily, but as my brain built up its chess pattern-recognition skills it became more of an even contest. Take time away from playing and I get 'rusty' – the brain doesn't fire up so quickly, and it's the same when you think about any skill you build and then take time away from. If patterns become redundant then we'll become sloppier at spotting them because the neuronal connections dedicated to them cease to fire together.

I'll never know whether the training my brain received through our chess evenings influenced my development as a therapist, but as I gained experience I became more and more aware of recognising patterns in the problems that clients presented me with. Not one-size-fits-all patterns in the traditional style of 'this is what smokers do, so you do this', but simply the fact that clients' problems emerged as a pattern, unique to them in its detail, but common in its composition. From that observation comes something fundamental to Cognitive Hypnotherapy – our job as therapists is to hunt *patterns*; the limiting patterns that form the problem state, and useful patterns that the client has that can be harnessed to the cause of problem relief.

Problems exist in time; they have a beginning, middle and an end. Problem thoughts are experienced in particular ways that can be described, and problems are identified by the brain as such because of perceived connections with previous experiences. These distinctions can all be mapped, and they need to be, because the greater our understanding of the way clients create the perception of their problem, the greater opportunity we have to influence that perception.

The quality of your questions will be a key feature in your success in this first phase of therapy. Clients will bombard you with information if you have rapport with them and listen for the right things. Neuro-Linguistic Programming has given us a tool that is invaluable for hunting the pattern with the client; the information his or her mind is using, usually unconsciously, to create his/her model of the world. It is called the meta-model. If you are unfamiliar with it you'll find an explanation in Appendices 4 and 5. I suggest you read it after you've completed Part I for the first time.

Context

Let's turn to consideration of the first three constituents of a problem pattern (we come to consequence later).

Two brothers were raised by an abusive alcoholic father who beat them regularly and took pleasure in humiliating and belittling them. When they grew to manhood one brother became the image of his father and treated his children every bit as badly. The other brother grew into a successful businessman and loving father. Someone asked each in turn, 'How did you manage to turn out this way?'

Both gave the same answer, 'How could I have turned out any differently given my childhood?'

Context is about 'why and when' we know something. It is not the things that happen to us that define us, it is what we decide those things mean to us that are crucial. Because Cognitive Hypnotherapy does not believe in there being a 'true' version of reality out there to find – there is no objective truth – then the individual meaning we give to things is a critical point of leverage in changing a problem pattern. While regression is the most powerful way that I've found to re-contextualise a client's experience, it's often not enough on its own. Reframing the past needs to be supported by moving that change in the way we look at the past into how we perceive the present, and how we can then imagine the future. All three time frames need to be connected together. If the original negative event is the *cause* of the present problem (its *effect*) then releasing the negative meaning from that event creates a new cause that the brain can use to calculate a different (better) present. In this book we're going to concentrate on how suggestion can assist this process effectively.

In terms of information gathering, context questions are about

'Why this, now?' Essentially we are searching for the criterion that causes the brain to make a pattern match between a present situation and a memory thread within the individual's matrix. To do this we ask questions that cause the client to calibrate differences in a variety of ways, i.e.:

> Do you always have this problem?
> Are there times when it's worse or better?
> What's different about those times?
> Have you always had this problem?
> What was different about you before you had it?
> What was happening in your life when this problem started?
> What is happening in your life when you have this problem that is similar to when the problem began?

Clearly each problem will require a different combination of these questions, and the client's response to them will dictate the direction you go in. As a rough guide these next two categories of context questions provide the principles of what you're looking to learn. One searches for the similarities that define the problem, the other searches for differences or exceptions, which also define the problem (think of the algorithms $A = B$ and $A = $ not B).

Context mapping

This category is looking for the boundaries of the problem; how far does it extend, how similar do things or situations need to be before they get lumped in with the problem; how consistent is the response?

> 'When he looked over your shoulder you got the feeling you call nervous.'

'Yes.'
'Do you know where in your body you get that feeling?'
'Yes, here [indicating stomach].'
'Keep that feeling for a moment. Are there other situations that make you feel the same way?'
[Thinks for a moment] 'Yes, when my wife inspects the decorating I'm doing.'
'And when else...?', etc.

Here we are exploring similarities to establish the pattern – the matrix that contains the belief 'I am not confident.'

The questions above will help to keep you focused on the important question you need to keep asking yourself: **'What do I need to know at this moment to help this client?'** If you can't answer that question in relation to the one you're asking then be careful, you may be losing yourself in the story.

Exception mapping

It has been my experience that no matter how chronic the problem is, there are always times when it doesn't happen. For example, take confidence problems. I have never met anybody who had **no** confidence, **all** the time. If they're out there they probably can't make it to therapy. Like many other problems, issues about confidence and competence are context dependent, and it can be useful to map the exceptions because it gives you an idea of the scale of the problem, and it gives you the opportunity to observe any common link between contexts that equal confidence, and contexts that don't.

1 What is different about the times when...(you have confidence, get along, remain calm)? Assume the attitude that you as a therapist would be surprised if there were no exceptions.

2 How do you get that to happen? This question suggests to the client that he/she is responsible for this difference, it didn't 'just happen'. Once they identify how they got something to be different they have the beginning of the means to do it again. It might also bring up rationalisations that reveal the limiting beliefs that underpin the problem: 'I didn't panic then because my friend was with me. He always knows what to do.' (Limiting belief = I won't know what to do/get it right.) 'I felt confident because it was my friends I was talking to.' ('Not friends' = danger.)

3 How does it make your day go differently when...(the exception happens)? This helps the client trace the C>E relationships between the problem and his/her life as a whole, and to become aware of the Butterfly Effect (see Glossary) a small positive can make on their life.

4 Who else noticed when you...(were feeling confident, got along, remained calm)? How could you tell? This question will often serve to send their awareness away from their self, and onto others, which is usually helpful. It also focuses them on behaviour that is reinforced by the approval of others.

5 Have you ever had this problem before? If yes: How did you resolve it then? What would you need to do to get that to happen again? This question will often identify successful behaviours that have lapsed. What often happens when people consciously overcome a problem is they

gradually revert to their former behaviours as their attention drifts. Because they may not be aware of this, the return of the behaviour can be interpreted as it being part of their status quo: 'It's just the way I am.'

6 What do you do that you enjoy? Any hobbies or interests? Do you have your problem when you're doing x (hobby or interest)? We often have skills and attitudes in successful endeavours that could be used in other contexts.

Generally speaking the more tightly contextualised the problem the briefer will be the therapy. Broader contexts often, but not always, take longer to disrupt the problem pattern.

At this point I'm going to pretend a session with a client goes in a linear sequence of questions where I first ask about context, then structure, then process. In reality no such thing occurs, the questioning goes in all directions based on what emerges from the client, but if I provided a real transcript at this point it would appear very confusing and I'd probably lose myself in the explanation. So, Helen's been waiting patiently, let me explore the context of her problem:

After the settling-in questions – 'Did you find me okay?' etc., and the opportunity to establish rapport – I'll usually begin with a simple open question like:

T: What can I help you with?
H: It's everything, really. I just seem to get stuck with everything.
T: Can you give me some examples?
H: Well, at work I know I'm capable of more but something just holds me back. I've got an exam coming up and I panic every time I think about it.
T: Have you always felt this way?
H: Pretty much. I scraped through at school even though I should have done better. I always get this feeling that people think I'm stupid.
T: Can you remember a specific time recently when you got this feeling?
H: ...Yes, I had to give a presentation to my boss and some of my colleagues. It wasn't even about anything important.
T: And what happened?
H: When I stood up my mind went blank and I thought I was going to pass out. I just wanted to run out of the room I was so scared. Now every time I think about doing something like it I feel sick.
T: And as you remember being so scared, if you could point in your body to where you get that feeling, where would you point?
H: [Indicates chest] Here, and my face feels really hot.
T: Right, so as you feel that feeling, are there other times when you get that feeling?

H: ...Yes, every time I took my driving test...meeting new people....
T: Good. And are there ever times when you're with people and this doesn't happen?
H: Oh yes, when I'm with my friends I'm happy to speak up – in fact they can't believe I have this problem. Also I play netball and I shout my head off on the court.
T: What's different?
H: I don't know...I guess my friends don't judge me...and I know I'm good at netball.
T: Are you ever comfortable with people who you feel are judging you?
H: ...No...I can't think of any.
T: Does this have an effect on relationships?
H: Oh totally! I hate dating because I get in such a state, worrying about saying the right thing, whether they'll like me. It's a complete nightmare.
T: Are you in a relationship right now?
H: Yes, Mark. We've been going out for about a year.
T: Do you get that feeling with him?
H: Not any more. I did the first couple of months but it's easier now.
T: What made it easier?
H: Well, he's just very sweet and patient and I kind of relaxed with him.

That's a distilled taste of context and exception mapping. As I said earlier, in a real session these questions would be wrapped in conversation and you'll see later that I would have diverted along different process-and-structure subject areas as they arose, so it wouldn't have seemed so staccato. We'll add these in as we go. Let's pause Helen again and look at the next part of pattern hunting.

Structure

The way we think is unique. It is one of the great mistakes of human communication that has us think that the way you experience the world around you is the same way that I do. It is the basis of a lot of heartache and discord because when we see people respond in a situation differently from the way we would we often label that difference negatively – they're being stubborn, difficult, stupid etc. After all, if their way was the right way surely we'd be responding in that way too? We're not, so they must be wrong.

By this stage of the book we know that the way we respond has everything to do with the firing patterns in the brain, but we have yet to look at the subjective way we experience these patterns of neurons – how can we describe the qualities of our thoughts?

Go and ask half a dozen people if they think in black and white or colour and watch as they struggle for a second to think. Then ask them if they've ever thought of that question before? Most of them won't have. Had you? We all know that we think, but most of us don't know how we think. This is what I'm talking about as *structure*; how is the client aware of the problem? Does he/she *see* an internal representation (a picture)? Is that picture in black and white or colour? If it's black and white does changing it to colour make a difference to how he/she feels about the problem? Where in the body does he/she feel the emotion that goes with the problem? Can it be moved, and, if it can, does that make a difference?

These differences in the way we experience our thoughts have been identified by NLP and are known as submodalities (SMDs). The term just derives from the use of the word 'modality' to denote one of our senses – thus visual is a modality, as is auditory. SMDs are the building blocks of each modality, so if the visual qualities of a memory include it being pictured in two dimensions or three, or as a movie or a still picture, these are visual SMDs; the tone of a remembered voice, and where in your head it seems to originate from are auditory SMDs, and so on. Now for the weird part. What the pioneers of NLP discovered was that not all SMDs are equal. Some appear to be key in the meaning of the thought, so changing them will cause a shift in the effect of the thought in the individual. So if, for example, a client gets into a cold sweat whenever he thinks of talking to someone new, you question him to discover the SMDs of that thought (we'll stick to visual for simplicity's sake) and he sees it in colour, through his own eyes (associated). It's a movie rather than a still picture, and he sees the picture close up and in the lower right quadrant of his visual field etc. For this thought, as for all others, there will be one or more of these SMDs that is key to the meaning of the thought. Changing one or more of them will alter the experience the person has about the thought, changing any of the others won't. So in this case, getting the client to experiment by changing the visual SMDs one at a time and asking whether it makes the thought feel better, worse, or the same will identify one or more that make the thought feel better.

These key SMDs are known as drivers and are great bits of information to obtain from the client to include later in your suggestions.

> An important thing to remember is that the drivers are individual to each person, and may be different for each person from one thought to another.

The main SMDs are listed below. There are others but the ones I've included are the ones that people report most often.

VISUAL

    Black and White or Colour
    Near or Far
    Bright or Dim
    Location
    Size of Picture
    Associated or Dissociated
    Focused or Defocused
    Framed or Panoramic
    Movie or Still
    Movie – Fast/Normal/Slow
    3D or Flat

AUDIO

    Location
    Internal or External
    Loud or Soft
    Fast or Slow
    High or Low (pitch)
    Cadence (rhythm)
    Duration

KINAESTHETIC

    Location
    Size
    Shape
    Intensity
    Duration
    Pressure
    Heat
    Weight

So structure is about 'how we know' something. Do you prefer spaghetti Bolognese to curry? How do you know? What's more important to you, fun or security? According to NLP it is the SMD driver qualities of the thoughts you have in response to those questions that define your answer, and changing the SMD qualities of those thoughts will change the meaning of them. I've found that to be true – the trick is getting the change to stick, but more on that later.

While we each tend to focus on a particular modality, our 'knowing' something tends to be a whole-body experience – we 'feel' something is right or wrong at the same time as seeing/hearing/smelling/tasting the evidence. In Cognitive Hypnotherapy we question to identify in as much detail as possible the SMD qualities of the clients' problem pattern in all modalities. I believe Richard Bandler has been quoted as saying that if you strip everything else away what you are left with are SMDs, so they are worth the time you invest in learning to listen and hunt for them. They may be the bridge between the language of the brain – the hiss and bubble of chemical and electrical activity – and the language we communicate to the world with.

If we return to Helen and look at the interview with her again we can add some SMD elicitation questions.

> T: Can you remember a specific time recently when you got this feeling?
> H: ...Yes, I had to give a presentation to my boss and some of my colleagues. It wasn't even about anything important.
> T: And what happened?
> H: When I stood up my mind went blank and I thought I was going to pass out. I just wanted to run out of the room, I was so scared. Now every time I think about doing something like it I feel sick.

> T: When you think of doing something like it again, do you get an image?
> H: ...Yes, I see myself making a pig's ear of it again.
> T: And is that picture close or far away?
> H: I hadn't really thought of it...er, it's really close, in my face.
> T: And is it black and white or colour?
> H: It's colour.
> T: And as you look at that picture are you in it or looking at it through your own eyes?
> H: Through my own eyes.

The above is a sample of visual SMD qualities. Knowing that these qualities contribute to the anticipation of the 'pig's ear' will later give us some ideas about how to create suggestions to transform her anticipation of a similar situation.

> T: What was the feeling of passing out?
> H: Er...well, my breathing got really tight.
> T: And as you remember being so scared, if you could point in your body to where you get that feeling, where would you point?
> H: [Indicates chest] Here, and my face feels really hot.
> T: And if that feeling had a shape, what shape would it be?
> H: Oh, a kind of band around my chest.
> T: Is that a wide or a narrow band?
> H: It's wide.
> T: Does it have a feeling to it?
> H: Yes, it's really tight.

Similarly these questions identify some of the kinaesthetic SMDs of Helen's experience. If she didn't feel them how would it affect her experience?

> T: Are you in a relationship right now?
> H: Yes, Mark. We've been going out for about a year.
> T: Do you get that feeling with him?
> H: Not any more. I did the first couple of months but it's easier now.
> T: What made it easier?
> H: Well, he's just very sweet and patient and I've kind of relaxed with him.
> T: How is that relaxed feeling different from the tight feeling in your chest?
> H: It's lower down, like a warmth in my stomach.
> T: Anything else?
> H: Well, it's just a slower feeling – I know that sounds silly, but when I'm scared the feeling in my chest is really fast.

This provides a contrast between different states. It gives us a way of knowing what her feeling of the problem isn't. Later we'll talk about how to utilise this in suggestion.

Process

Time is that great gift of nature which keeps everything from happening at once.
L. J. Overbeck

If context is about 'why and when we know' something, and

structure is about 'how we know' something, then process is about 'how we do' something. We think of time as something fixed and immutable, but our perception of time is very subjective. When investigating a client's process we are concerned with mapping the progress of his/her problem pattern from its initial firing until its return to stasis. In Wordweaving™ we use two models to achieve this mapping – the matrix model (MM), which traces the steps between stimulus, response and return to stasis – and Neuro-logical Levels, which track the levels of interaction between the environment and the self. The latter will be utilised later – first let me show you how the MM can shed light on Helen's problem.

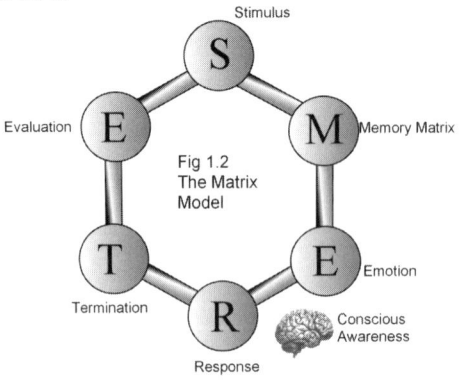

Fig 1.2
The Matrix Model

T: Can you remember a specific time recently when you got this feeling?
H: ...Yes, I had to give a presentation to my boss and some of my colleagues. It wasn't even about anything important.
T: And what happened?
H: When I stood up my mind went blank and I thought I was going to pass out. I just wanted to run out of the room, I was so scared. Now every time I think about doing something like it I feel sick.

T: On a scale of nought to ten, where ten is the worst, how strong was that feeling?
H: Easily a ten.
T: Good, so what was it that triggered your mind going blank? Take me back to that moment.
H: Let's think...I was shuffling my papers trying to stay calm and then my boss announced my name and what my presentation was about. So I stood up and looked around and everyone was looking at me. I remember thinking 'Oh God!' and I froze. I must have looked like a rabbit caught in headlights.
T: And as you froze what were you feeling?
H: Absolutely terrified, I really thought I would pass out.
T: So you saw all of their eyes on you and you felt terrified...what did you do?
H: I tried to talk but it was pretty obvious to everyone that I wasn't right, so I apologised and said I felt ill and went off to the toilet.
T: How quickly did you feel better?
H: Well, I felt absolutely sick in the loo, but then Tricia came and said the meeting was over and they'd rescheduled my input and I felt instant relief.
T: And what did you think about what had happened afterwards?
H: I really beat myself up. They must have thought me so stupid; no way would they have believed I was ill.

So, in MM terms the sequence of her problem pattern in this instance runs something like:

> **Stimulus:** Attention on her (context mapping would provide the information about whose eyes cause this response and whose don't).
> **Memory matrix:** Questioning won't retrieve this bit of information, regression will.
> **Emotion:** Terror, scared.
> **Response:** Avoidance – makes excuse and leaves.
> **Termination:** When giving the talk is postponed.
> **Evaluation:** Conscious evaluation is self-loathing. What she reports is a likely example of the *therapeutic paradox* – the point of the problem pattern is likely to be about avoiding failure, but the pattern instead creates it. (See Appendix 1.) Helen's unconscious evaluation will be based on what it seeks to avoid. In all probability the problem is based on a premature evaluation of a childhood event. Because of this, her unconscious is likely to conclude that the problem process was successful in its aim – it prevented her from reliving the childhood significant emotional event (SEE).

Later, when we get to the stage of creating suggestions for Helen, you'll see how we use Neuro-logical Levels (NLLs) to organise them. Essentially the MM is about what kicks off the problem and then what the response is. In NLL terms this corresponds to environment – everything in the world we can be aware of that is not our central nervous system, including the feelings we feel in our body. This is where the stimulus will originate and the emotion will be experienced. The NLL level of behaviour corresponds to the MM stages of response and termination, and the NLL levels of belief or identity would be responsible for the MM stage of evaluation. You can think of the relationship between the two models as the MM mapping the action and mixture of our NLLs in specific situations.

Summarising Helen's problem state

So what have we learnt so far about Helen's problem pattern? What is her evidence for having the problem?

From the questions asked so far, and we're a long way from finished yet, we've identified that her problem seems to revolve around certain types of people who she thinks will find her stupid. These people tend to be people she is not close to or hasn't known for long. People in authority or in a position to judge her competence (i.e. stupid or not stupid) appear to be key. Any situation involving these people is anticipated as being scary.

Helen knows she's in one of these situations because her mind goes blank, she feels sick and it's as if she's going to faint. Her face feels hot and her chest as if strapped with a tight band. The feeling in her chest is 'fast'.

If she imagines the next time she has to face a situation like this the image is associated (through her own eyes), is close-up and in colour.

We don't yet know which, if any, of these are drivers, i.e. if we changed them, which would cause the future image to appear less terrifying. Her response to this feeling of fear is to flee. Afterwards she beats herself up about it.

There's plenty here to make my point. What do we do to begin moving Helen from this problem state? First we need to identify what she would need to see/hear/feel that would mean she's better; **her** *solution state*.

The Solution state: begin with the end in mind

Many counsellors and therapists begin to lose their way when therapy extends beyond four or five sessions, and it's easy to see why. The client presents with an issue that begins to shift in emphasis as the work progresses, other issues bubble to the surface, appointments get postponed, and all of a sudden you can't actually remember what the client wanted in the first place. The thing is, if you don't know what the client wants, and he/she doesn't either, when will you know when you've got there?

I remember being at a seminar a while ago and talking to a nice lady during coffee break who'd described herself as a transpersonal therapist. I wasn't sure quite what that meant so I was eager to find out about her approach. At a certain point I mentioned therapy coming to an end and a look of puzzlement came over her.

'End?' she said. 'But therapy never really ends, does it? It just transforms to another level.'

Does it? Surely some people who come to see me to stop biting their nails should be allowed to do so without signing up for a full spiritual makeover?

Someone once said, and by the time I've finished this book I may have remembered who it was (it's my age): 'Everyone needs therapy, but most don't need very much.'

That is a view I completely subscribe to. Get them in, help them get what they came for, and get them out. So therapy begins with finding out exactly what they want, and their *evidence procedure for having achieved it* – how will they know when they've got it? The following is a framework of questions that can be very helpful in establishing this starting point.

Defining their outcome

It is vital that the outcome of therapy is always clear, and the goals of the client should be established at the outset and revisited regularly as therapy progresses. Many people will begin by telling you what they don't want:

'I don't want to feel depressed anymore.' Or, 'I don't want to keep having bad relationships.'

The first step in treatment planning is to find out what the client wants instead of what he/she has now. The goal must be expressed as a positive, otherwise you can both go off in directions based on different assumptions.

Questions for attainable outcomes

Where are you now?
This is what we've just covered, the questions about context, structure and process that identified the *problem state*.

What do you want?
'If I could wave a magic wand and you had what you wanted from coming here today how would you know? What would be different?'

This causes clients to search for their evidence criteria for being better. Mostly they won't have thought of this because their attention is tuned to the problem, not to what is 'not the problem'. This question begins to re-tune them. Just as their problem is a pattern, so will their solution state be once they achieve it. We need to know what they can imagine of it to begin with so we can start to suggest it into existence. At this moment the structure part of the solution pattern should be possible to imagine because it's almost certain that they will have felt the feeling they want to have at some point in their life. For example, with Helen:

> T: If I could wave a magic wand and you had what you wanted from coming here today how would you know? What would be different?
>
> H: Well, I'd be with someone – or a bunch of people like that time with my boss, and I'd feel confident.
>
> T [Meta-model time]: And how would you know you were feeling confident?
>
> H: For a start my hands wouldn't be sweaty, my face wouldn't be hot and I wouldn't feel I was going to be sick or faint.

Notice how she's focusing on kinaesthetic SMDs. Also, Helen's telling me what she doesn't want to feel – which is valuable, but it's easier to move her attention onto something else she **can** notice, rather than create a non-awareness of the negative pattern. So I continue to question:

> T: What would you feel instead?
>
> H: Oh…I hadn't thought of that, I've felt this way for so long.
>
> T: Sure. How about those times when you are confident with people? Would how you feel then be a good way to feel in the situation we're talking about?
>
> H: Oh yes, of course. When I'm with my friends I feel…easy.
>
> T: How does 'easy' feel?
>
> H: Nice. It's like when I feel warm and cosy…safe.
>
> T: How's your breathing? Do you breathe in the same way?

> H: Um...no. When I'm panicking my breathing is short and high in my chest, almost like I'm panting. When I'm relaxed my breathing is slower and kind of sits in my stomach. Funny...I hadn't thought of that.
> T: Excellent. Anything else about how your body feels when you're relaxed and confident?
> H: ...Yes. My energy! When I'm with my friends I feel bubbly and....almost excited. When I'm panicking I feel like a little mouse – like I don't want people to notice me.
> T: Brilliant. Anything else?
> H: ...No...I think that's the main things that come to mind.

Notice how again Helen's focus is mainly kinaesthetic evidence. We have a consistency that will lead the focus of our suggestions when we take this information and begin to create them. Before we do we also have NLLs to help us.

Future pacing using Neuro Logical Levels

The more clearly your clients can imagine themselves in their future as the persons they would be without their problem, the more information you will have to wordweave via post-hypnotic suggestions that prime their unconscious mind to fulfil their evidence criteria – it's like placing the clients' idealised self into their future and then setting their unconscious to begin to guide them towards it, bringing to the foreground of their attention whatever moves them forward, whatever confirms the emergence of this new pattern, and keep in the background everything that formed the evidence of the old.

NLLs are one of the most useful models to come from NLP. I'm aware of criticism of it, that it isn't consistent with the system of logical levels as posited by Gregory Bateson. To be honest, I've never really followed the argument through because, for me, NLP is about things that are useful, not whether they are given a name that is semantically accurate.

I explained the principles of NLL in the previous book, if you need a quick refresher I've included one as Appendix 2.

In this context Dilts' model is used to identify the client's evidence criteria throughout each level. The principle can be used in two ways; eyes wide open as part of a standard question-asking session, or as part of a more hypnotic exercise. The first version goes like this:

ENVIRONMENT

'If you didn't have this issue any longer, what would be different in your life? Describe what you would like in your life without your problem.'

BEHAVIOUR

'What would you be doing that you currently aren't?' 'What would you like to do that you currently can't?'

CAPABILITIES

'What strengths or resources do you have that will help you let go of your problem?' 'What strengths or resources would you like to have that would help you let go of your problem?'

Beliefs

'If this problem were gone, what would you believe about yourself that you don't completely believe now?'

Values

'If this problem were to disappear what would become really important to you?'

Identity

'If you could say something about yourself that would be true when you've let go of this problem – begin it with 'I am' – what would you say?'

If you choose to use it within a hypnotic session then, at whatever point you think appropriate and with the client in trance it could go something like:

'If you were to imagine going out into the future to whenever you have what you came here for...we can both be curious about all the things that have changed...so that if you were to be open to everything around you in the future that means you have what you want...what would you see around you? [client answers] and what would you feel?

'And it might surprise you to see all the new things you're doing...the differences people can see in the way you behave...and as you begin to enjoy seeing yourself in this new way just tell me the things you notice most....

'Because to behave in new ways so often means we've developed new resources, skills and abilities...or made stronger those we already had...for you to be behaving in this new way in the future what are those capabilities you see in your new self that make it possible?

'And it can be such a good thing to realise how when things change so can the things we value...things that we might not have realised the true importance of...or that simply weren't present in the life of who you once were...so as you look at the person you're becoming...what's important to him/her?

'And what does he/she believe about him/herself that makes all this possible?

'If there was something you believe in the future, which by believing it means that you're living now as you most want to...what is it?

'So if you were to look at yourself in the mirror and see this future you looking back...and he/she said something beginning with 'I' that truly describes him/her what would it be?'

As you can see, in either case the purpose is to have the client consider change at all the levels that create and support it. The words he/she uses to describe these changes are the criteria against which they will be measured as therapy progresses. This is good news because with these questions we know what to suggest that will tune the mind to perceive these changes occurring. In Helen's case I'm using the questions as part of the first-session information gathering, but there would be nothing wrong about using the hypnotic version as part of a first trance experience to round the session off with. Let's see what Helen comes up with:

ENVIRONMENT

T: If you didn't have this issue any longer, what would be different in your life? Describe what you would like in your life without your problem.

H: My relationship with my boyfriend will be even better. Even though I feel comfortable with him I'm still aware I hold back from him. I've never let anyone really close to me. So there'll be that, real intimacy. At work...God! If I was more confident I think the sky's the limit. I can see how I could really go a long way.

Behaviour

T: What would you be doing differently?
H: Well, I'd probably look for opportunities to get myself noticed. I'd be a bit more aggressive – well assertive anyway – in saying what I thought was right. So often I can see we're making a mistake but I'm scared to say anything.

Capabilities

T: And for you to be confident in this way what capabilities would you need that you don't think you have right now?
H [Thinks]: Mainly determination. I tend to give in too easily at the moment. To be confident I'd need to stick with what I believe to be right.
T: And what resources do you have in other situations that would be useful when you want to have confidence?
H: Well, I think my friends would say I'm quite quick – I pick things up quickly.

Beliefs

T: So when you have this confidence, what would you believe about yourself that you don't completely believe now?
H: Oh, believing that I was good enough, that I'm as good as anyone else.
T: Good. And when you imagine the 'you' in the future with this confidence, what do you imagine would be important to you? (Values.)
H: To be worthy of respect, that if I'm going to make a noise about myself that I make sure I'm worth listening to.

Identity

T: So if, in the future, you had all those things – you had created all these differences in your life. As the 'you' in the future looks in the mirror at herself, if she were to say something about her that summed herself up, beginning with 'I' what would it be?
H: Something like I said earlier: 'I am good enough.' No! How about 'I'm worthy.'

Finally there are some questions on ecology – i.e. how will change in her life affect everything else connected to it? Remember the old adage: 'Be careful what you wish for, you may just get it'? These questions are designed to make sure another problem doesn't supplant this one.

T: Is this change only for you?
H: I know it sounds selfish but yes, it is mainly. I mean, my boyfriend will benefit, but he seems happy as things are so I'm not doing it for him.
T: What will it mean to him for you to have more confidence?
H: Um, well, like I said, I'll be free to be more open, intimate. I can start to take more of a part in the decisions we make.
T: So what will you gain by getting what you came here for?
H: My freedom! No, seriously, actually freedom's quite close to what I mean. Being free to take control of my life and make it what I want.
T: And what might you lose by getting what you came here for?
H: My bloody inhibitions. My stupid fear of being discovered as a fraud. The whole being-scared, feeling-sick thing.
T: Anything you might lose by being confident that you'd like to keep?
H: Oh...maybe my boyfriend. I suppose he might feel threatened by my not being the demure girl he's with now. But if he wouldn't like me that way then he's not right for me anyway.

In a short space of time you can see how much information can be gained. If we mapped out both problem state and solution states we'd have this:

Problem State

- Certain types of people make her think they will find her stupid.
- These people tend to be people she is not close to or hasn't known for long.
- People in authority or in a position to judge her competence (i.e. stupid or not stupid) appear to be key. Any situation involving these people is anticipated as being scary.
- Helen knows she's in one of these situations because her mind goes blank, she feels sick and it's as if she's going to faint.
- Her face feels hot and her chest like it's strapped with a tight band.
- The feeling in her chest feels 'fast'.
- If she imagines the next time she has to face a situation like this the image is associated (through her own eyes), is close up and in colour.
- Her response to this feeling of fear is to flee.
- Afterwards she beats herself up about it.

Solution State

- Helen's relationship with her boyfriend will be more intimate with no holding back.
- At work she wouldn't feel there were any limitations to how far she could go.
- She'd look for opportunities to get herself noticed and be more assertive.
- She would speak up if she didn't agree with something.
- She would feel determined and be able to use the fact that she can pick up things quickly.
- She would feel worthy of respect and know that she's as good as anyone else.
- She could look at herself in the mirror and be able to say "I'm worthy" and mean it.
- In situations that used to be a problem she would now be easy and safe, her breathing would be slower and down in her stomach and she would have a bubbly energy that she has with her friends

This is plenty of information to create an initial suggestion pattern aimed at beginning to tune Helen's mind to bring the solution-state evidence to the foreground and relegate the problem-state info to the background.

With people new to Wordweaving™ I suggest that they make the first session with a client purely an information-gathering exercise – with perhaps an induction to calibrate the responsiveness of the client. When still learning Wordweaving™ it can be a lot of pressure to think you have to listen to a client and then instantly be able to create a suggestion pattern based on the information he/she has given you. It is possible with practice, but in the early days give yourself space. Book the second session for a week later and then sit down in between and create the suggestion pattern. Think of the first session as the one where you're figuring out where to tap, and the second one where you bring out the hammer.

How quickly you help a client will depend on how quickly you learn about his/her mind. That will depend on the quality of the questions you ask. The principle behind all questions should be,

> What do I need to know or say at this moment that will move my client most towards his/her outcome?

Let's look at questions themselves more deeply.

Chapter 2

Questions are the answer

Who says? Very clever, but just remember nobody likes a smart Alec. And who was Alec? Not a good start to this chapter, you might think, because that question clearly is not its own answer. So what kind of question is? Good – already we're into different classes of questions we can ask our clients, because not all questions are good ones. This chapter is specifically about how to frame suggestions as questions using presuppositions, in order to get their mind to anticipate what it might notice, that by doing so will make it realise things are getting better. It's also about what to do when a client says 'I can't do that,' 'I don't know,' 'My mind is blank!' – you know, one of those kinds of days.

I once heard the US hypnotherapist Kevin Hogan say that eighty per cent of all dialogue between a client and therapist should come from the client, and I think he's absolutely right. I also think that, outside of when you are making suggestions with the client in trance, eighty per cent of what comes out of your mouth should be questions – good questions, so that their eighty per cent contribution is useful. So what makes a good question? We've already covered questions that categorise the clients' problem and establish their outcome. They're good. This chapter is about how you phrase questions that cause the client to search within him/herself for an answer that is useful. The basis of this question form is something I covered in *Wordweaving*™ Volume I – presuppositions.

As you know language is a filter that reduces the information we need to communicate down to a manageable level. Presuppositions are one of the ways it accomplishes this. They cause the listener to make assumptions in order to make sense of the sentence the presupposition appears in. For example, if I say I'm sitting in the middle of the room it assumes there is a room, it has parts that aren't the middle, sides, ceiling, etc., that I exist, as does everything that isn't me and the room. It also presupposes that there are other things I could be doing in the middle of the room other than sitting. Phew. You can see that without our inherent ability to make assumptions based on presuppositions, communicating the simplest of things would take longer than anyone's patience. This ability is so unconscious that we are usually not even aware of it and the way it can influence us. How often have washing powders been re-launched as 'new and improved'? How bad must they have been when they first came on the market? But advertisers recognise that certain words – known as adverb or adjective modifiers – make things seem more attractive. Out of these pairs, which sounds more appealing?

A Flame grilled Aberdeen Angus steak
B A piece of cooked dead cow

A An approved main dealer
B Bert's Car Mart

A Pre-owned
B Second-hand

We cannot avoid being influenced by language, and often we are influenced without even knowing it. That is why presuppositional questioning can be so powerful. I can't do better than the following quotation to describe what we are trying to achieve when using them.

> What is the question that I can ask which by the very nature of the presuppositions in the question itself will cause the client to make the greatest amount of change by having to accept the presuppositions inherent in the question?
>
> Tad James, 1992[4]

That sentence probably needs reading several times to get its full meaning. I think it took me several years but it has become a cornerstone of my philosophy. If you really get the idea that you're helping your clients most when you're not making statements or giving them your ideas to solve their problem, but asking questions that engage their own creativity, you'll never get stuck with a client again.

What I'm going to do is present a question structure based on the presuppositional use of the algorithms $C > E$ (cause and effect) and $A = B$ (complex equivalence) that demonstrates the principle of using the client's mind to find the answer. First let me give an example of how many therapists deal with a situation:

> **Client:** The exam next week is going to be a nightmare, I know I'll freeze and my mind will go blank.
> **Direct therapist** making hypnotic suggestions later: *Next week you'll walk into the exam room and you'll feel confident. You know you've done the work and you know you can answer the questions easily. As you sit at your desk you look around and see everyone else is more nervous than you and that makes you feel relaxed.*

As you can see the therapist is supplying the answers from his or her own model of the world. In effect what this means is that the therapist is putting on the client's head and saying 'How would I be in this situation if I was better?' One of the most common mistakes we make as human beings is to think that people think as we do, so our ideas about their situation will automatically work for them too. It's why we get so exasperated when friends (and especially our children) don't take our advice. Also the therapist has used the word 'will'. In NLP this is called a modal operator of necessity. In terms of its use in suggestion it becomes a prediction that allows little leeway. If the client walks into the exam room next week and doesn't feel confident, or knows he/she hasn't really done the work, or has doubts as to ease of answering, or is surrounded by confident-looking people, then the possibility exists that the client's unconscious may do the calculation that [the suggestion] isn't true so hypnosis didn't work (C>E), and everything else the therapist has worked to achieve may unravel as a consequence. The client will experience the exam as he/she always has. It's not that direct suggestions are wrong *per se*, but the less involved the client is in creating what is suggested then the greater the risk that what is suggested won't be actualised. Remember the idea of Orr's Law I referred to in Volume I (p26)? Doctor Leonard Orr suggested we imagine the mind has two components, the Thinker and the Prover. The rule that comes from this is,

> what the Thinker thinks the Prover proves,
>
> not
>
> what I (the therapist) think you should think your prover will prove.

A variation of this is where the therapist assumes personal indirectness but is still working from his/her head and not the client's.

Client: The exam next week is going to be a nightmare, I know I'll freeze and my mind will go blank.
Therapist: *How would you like to feel instead?* (Good question!)
Client: I'd like to feel easy in myself so I can focus.
Therapist making hypnotic suggestions later: *So as you walk into the exam room you know you'll feel easy because your palms won't be sweaty and your breathing will be steady. All you'll be aware of as you sit at the table is the exam paper, you'll be so focused that nothing around you will disturb your concentration.*

That is better because at least the client has been asked for his evidence – *focus* and *feeling easy* – but then the therapist has fallen into the trap again of supplying his version of how he would know he's got that evidence. In NLP a key saying is that words are not the thing they represent; the *word* cat is not the same thing as *a* cat. Similarly a word that a client uses to describe something – like focus – has a particular meaning that is unique to him or her. In Appendix 3 I mention the idea of *surface* and *deep* structure. If you're unfamiliar with the concept have a look. In this instance the word 'focus' is a surface structure, and it is connected to his deep structure wherein lie all the associations, beliefs and experiences associated with that word. No two people will share the deep structure of any word – this is where so much confusion arises in communication. What has happened with this therapist is that he has taken the client's surface structure evidence for the solution state, and then delved into his own deep structure and created suggestions based on what the experience of feeling easy and focused would be for him.

Instead, asking the client for his/her deep structure takes the guesswork out of it for you:

Therapist: *So if you were in the exam room feeling easy and focused how would you know? (What is your deep-structure evidence for your surface-structure evidence?)*
Client: Well, I suppose my hands would be steady – they normally tremble when I'm nervous, and I wouldn't have a lump in my stomach. And when I started reading the questions I would feel calm and not keep jumping from one question to another looking for one I can answer.

The client here has focused mainly on what he/she wouldn't feel, and many do that. You have a choice of either asking what he would like to experience in its place – we'll ask him in a minute – or weave suggestions that cause him to search for it.

Therapist: *So your hands are steady, and if you had a feeling that lets you know you're feeling easy, what would that feeling be like?*
Client: Well, when I've had it in the past it's been a kind of warm feeling in my stomach and my chest feels easy – you know…to breathe.
Therapist: *Great, and if you knew what the feeling of calm would be that meant you could read the questions easily, what would that be like?*
Client: That's not so much a feeling – well it is – but I get the feeling because I don't have a voice in my head rushing me. Then there's just this feeling of quiet in my head.

This client is pretty helpful in his ability to provide detail – I picked him specially. Some won't, which is when we go back to Chapter 1 and ask more detailed *process* or *structure* questions, for example: 'If you get that feeling of calm in your body where would you point to it? If it had a shape what shape would it be? If it had a colour?' etc.

Assuming he's given the information provided above, a wordweaving pattern for him could be:

> **Therapist:** *And it might surprise you to realise how much easier your breathing is, and whether you notice it right away or later doesn't matter, it just means that the warmth that comes with feeling easy can spread through your stomach...and as your unconscious realises how this can help you really focus on the peace in your head that lets you read easily – one question at a time – passing so quickly because you know you can focus now on what's important.*

Let's pick that apart to see what's in it. Go through it and identify how it fulfils the three steps (aim, trance phenomena and linguistic framing) and compare it with what's below – no peeking!

> *And it might* – *it might* = modal operator of possibility. Words like *might, may*, and *can* offer less for the client to resist than *will* and avoid the pitfalls of prediction that were mentioned earlier.

> *surprise* – what I call a *guiding state*. We can't feel two competing states at the same time, so if a positive state is suggested for the moment when the client would normally experience something negative, like nervousness, then there's a good chance that the negative will be supplanted by the positive (the gestalt principle of foreground

and background). Other states include curiosity, anticipation, excitement and amusement.

you to realise – realise = presupposition of awareness. Any words that guide focus onto what the client could be aware of through his senses. In this case sense of feeling (kinaesthetic).

how much easier your breathing is – much easier = adverb/adjective modifier. As the name suggests this class of presuppositions modifies the listener's experience of another word in the sentence, either a noun or a verb. In this case it subtly guides his assessment of his breathing by getting him to measure the degree of ease, not the degree of difficulty i.e. 'Is it easier, or much easier?' Both, of course, would do. If you also put that it's the trance phenomena (TP) of sensory distortion, well done, it's creating a perception of his breathing that is suitable for the moment. In terms of the suggestion's aim, things within the body fall within the NLL of environment.

and whether you notice it – notice = another presupposition of awareness.

right away or later doesn't matter – or = a bind. Wonderfully useful. Also described as an exclusive/inclusive or. You create the illusion of the client having a choice, but whichever choice is made fulfils the desired outcome.

it just means that the warmth that comes with feeling easy – means = our friend, complex equivalence (A = B). This little word suggests a relationship between breathing easier and the feeling in his stomach growing. Such relationships don't have to be true causal connections – there's no real reason why a change of breathing should create the warmth in the stomach –they just have to be plausible. Just reading these things means your knowledge is growing. Read that sentence in the light of the one before it and you'll see that I just did the same thing to you. It doesn't have to mean that, but it's plausible.

can spread through your stomach – can = another modal operator of possibility. The feeling spreading could be a continuation of the earlier sensory distortion. The aim is again environment.

and as your unconscious realises – realises = presupposition of awareness.

how this can help you really focus on the peace in your head that lets you read easily = this sentence continues the flow of relationship from breathing – to a feeling of ease – to helping him focus. Again, plausible use of A = B. Also I've used his key word *focus* on another key word *peace*, so I bring a piece of his solution evidence to bear in an indirect way so it will probably occur that he focuses without realising he is. *Easily* modifies *read*, and the NLL aim is behaviour (read) and capability (read easily).

one question at a time – passing so quickly – time – passing = there are several terms for this, the most digestible of which is a run-on sentence. It's simply where two different ideas flow into one sentence by the use of a word that ends one idea and begins the second. In this case the word is *time*. Do I mean 'easily read one question at a time' or 'time passing so quickly'? Of course I intend to mean both, but leave it to the client's unconscious to take whatever meaning helps him most. I marked out the passage *one question at a time* to demonstrate how you could use an embedded command simply by subtly marking that portion out as different from the other words either side of it by a slight change of tone, or by looking away as you say it to alter the audio quality of it. The key to its success is subtlety. Finally, *time passing so quickly* is a TP of time distortion. Our perception of time is entirely subjective, it can fly or drag, we can notice its passing or it can go in a flash. Adjust it to fit the circumstances.

because you know – because = C > E the suggestion its use creates is that time will go quickly because he can focus on what's important. *You know* is the NLL of belief.

you can focus now on what's important – can = modal operator of possibility; *now* = presupposition of time; *what's important* = a lack of referential index – I'm not supplying what actually is important, I leave it to the client's unconscious to make sense of that. The appearance of the word *important* indicates an NLL of values.

The suggestion pattern incorporates the principle that roughly seventy per cent of suggestions should be aimed at environment, behaviour and capability, and then connected to a new belief or shift in values/identity by the use of C>E or A=B.

As you can see a lot can go into a little when you have the client provide the information and you use the elements present in Wordweaving™.

If we look again at the questions asked of the client you'll see there was a pattern to them:

> **Therapist:** *So your hands are steady, and if you had a feeling that lets you know you're feeling easy, what would that feeling be like?*
> **Therapist:** *Great, and if you knew what the feeling of calm would be that meant you could read the questions easily, what would that be like?*

The structure of the question is this:

> If you were able to do/have this (the solution state or anything that takes you towards it) how would you do it/how would you know?

The statement begins with the word *if*, which is a modal operator of *possibility*. In effect it says to the client, 'I'm not saying you can do this, but if you could?' It unconsciously reduces the pressure to come up with the 'right' answer and encourages him to play with possibilities. The rest of the sentence establishes a cause-and-effect relationship. 'If we were to get this desired *effect*, what would be your *cause* of it?'

Here are some uses of it:

1 If you could learn something, which by your learning it would mean you could let this problem go, what would you learn?

2 If there was one small thing you could begin to change that would mean you're getting better, what would you choose?

Notice how the slightly different phrasing creates a complex equivalence (A = B) rather than a cause and effect (C > E). The result is the same, so don't worry which one you use, the principle is that you're using the brain's own algorithms on itself. We talk in more depth about their use in Chapter 3.

3 **Therapist:** *If your anxiety had a colour what colour would it be? (A = B)*
   Client: 'Blue.'
   Therapist: *Great. If you were to make the colour brighter or darker which would make the anxiety smaller?*

This pattern sets up a complex equivalence of anxiety = blue. If we then use a bind, where the presuppositions inherent in the sentence cause the client to try out adjusting the SMD qualities of the colour, and calibrate on one of them making a difference, the chances are that it will. What happens if neither does? Great. You've discovered an SMD that isn't a driver, so you carry on until you find one that does, because at least one always will.

The key thing with each of these is that the wording causes the client to get the result, the therapist doesn't have to try to guess – e.g. 'The colour of anxiety is yellow, so make that yellow darker, so it feels better, doesn't it?'

It will still often remain your judgment about what you think the best effect for the client would be that you are asking him/

her to find the way of achieving – just do your best to make the effect be a result of the information the client's given you, and not take it from your own model of the world.

The second form of the question can be useful for clients with issues that overwhelm them in their scope, such as anorexia. The problem pattern of that condition tends to be complex and present in almost all areas of their life. The Ericksonian method of splitting – working on one small part until an improvement is noticed and linking that improvement to the next small part – can be very effective. It would be your choice as the therapist to decide on that approach, but your question would get the client to decide which is the best part to start with instead of your saying, 'Right, let's begin by getting your meal portions bigger.'

You could say something like, 'If there was some part of your approach to eating that we could start with, that by changing it would mean you're starting to change, what would you choose?'

Similarly with question three. It's your choice to use a visual SMD to ease the anxiety rather than a kinaesthetic one – based on the fact the client finds it easy to visualise, not the fact that it's the sense **you** find easiest to utilise. It remains the client's job to determine the colour and the change that works for her.

'Client-centred' approaches often conjure up the image of the client meandering over months or even years through her subjective experiences with her patient counsellor or therapist nodding gentle encouragement. Wordweaving™ is also a client-centred approach, but it involves more of an interplay between the therapist and the client. You have taken the client's history and you have a good idea of her problem pattern. You decide what objective is most likely to succeed in changing that pattern and then you phrase your questions so that the client finds a way to achieve that change.

You might be getting the feeling that the mind's algorithms have a big part to play in Cognitive Hypnotherapy, and you'd be right. A client's problems are based on the calculations the brain makes based on the three algorithms. To move her towards the solution we have to create new calculations – but use the same algorithms. A master of hypnotherapy gave me a huge insight into how to achieve this.

Chapter 3
The Boynian pattern

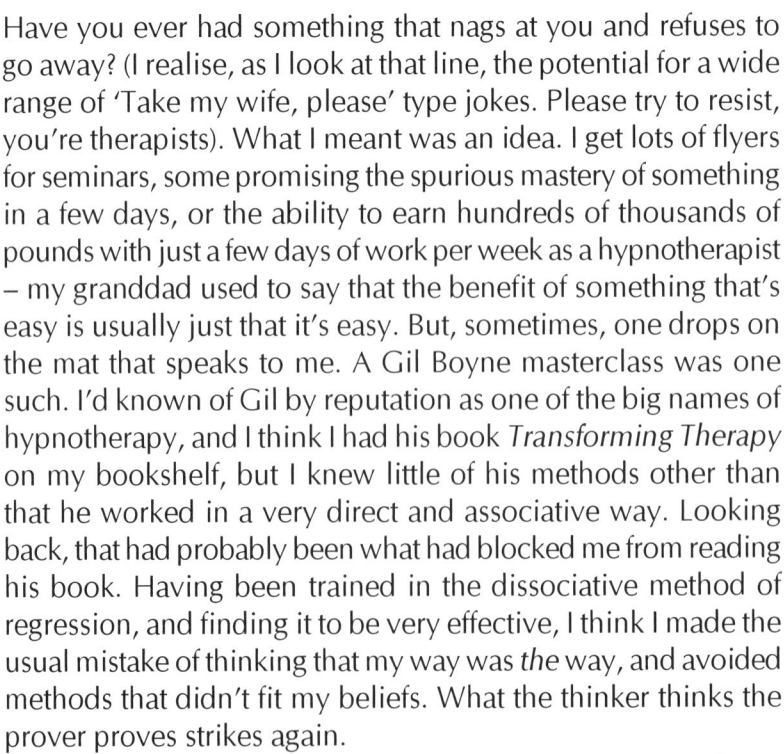

Have you ever had something that nags at you and refuses to go away? (I realise, as I look at that line, the potential for a wide range of 'Take my wife, please' type jokes. Please try to resist, you're therapists). What I meant was an idea. I get lots of flyers for seminars, some promising the spurious mastery of something in a few days, or the ability to earn hundreds of thousands of pounds with just a few days of work per week as a hypnotherapist – my granddad used to say that the benefit of something that's easy is usually just that it's easy. But, sometimes, one drops on the mat that speaks to me. A Gil Boyne masterclass was one such. I'd known of Gil by reputation as one of the big names of hypnotherapy, and I think I had his book *Transforming Therapy* on my bookshelf, but I knew little of his methods other than that he worked in a very direct and associative way. Looking back, that had probably been what had blocked me from reading his book. Having been trained in the dissociative method of regression, and finding it to be very effective, I think I made the usual mistake of thinking that my way was *the* way, and avoided methods that didn't fit my beliefs. What the thinker thinks the prover proves strikes again.

Yet something made me keep his flyer and I returned to it several times over the next few days with the whisper in my head, that I should go, getting louder. I was eight years into my practice and was tired of training other people's hypnotherapy courses. The idea of writing my own was really attracting me and my mind was open to learn something new – where better to look than the opposite of everything I'd held to be true?

So on the appointed day I turned up at Guy's Hospital with the feeling of anticipation that I love about the first day of a course. I suspect that Gil is someone you either like or you don't. He's a man who is very confident of his views and has the assurance that comes with over forty years of experience. He's direct with his clients and sees potency in the therapist as a necessary trait. It caused a lot of people in the audience of therapists and counsellors to suck on their teeth. His view is that people need to fully experience the negative emotion that has been holding them back in order to transform it into something positive – with his Christian beliefs this is usually love and forgiveness. To achieve that he is comfortable working through clients' abreactions, and won't even allow them to wipe the snot from their noses. It looks pretty hardcore, and it is. How I incorporated it into my style of regression is a story for another book (I tried, I really did. It just slipped out). What I am going to focus on now is a pattern I heard him use on his demonstration subjects at the seminar. Later, when I launched my hypnotherapy course, I kept noticing it as I showed videos of him to my students, until finally the full significance of it came to me as I wrote *The Science of Suggestion*. To give it its full significance I first need to go back over some things you may already be familiar with, I hope the feeling of déjà vu doesn't last too long.

You know that most of the processing done by the brain is for the purpose of making sense of the information flowing through our senses. In other words it devotes itself to seeking patterns of information around us that are either likely to cause us danger or to assist in our survival. A pattern of information could be anything from a sabre tooth tiger to a quarter pounder with cheese. Our ability to spot patterns is essential to our survival, and is present in everything we do.

Scientists talk of a thing called Occam's razor – how nature always reduces things to the simplest form. Our brain does the same thing for pattern recognition, and for the purposes of Wordweaving™ I've reduced what the brain does with incoming information down to three basic algorithms:

C > E	This is because of that
A = B	This is the same as that
A = not B	This is different from that

The labels given to the first two by NLP are cause and effect and complex equivalence. In Volume I you learnt how to use C > E, A = B and the suggestion of change or difference to create a shift in perception and to link changes in the client's awareness of his/her environment, behaviour and capabilities to an improved belief or sense of identity. Now, thanks to Gil's insight, I'm going to show you how to use C > E and A = B to obtain information from clients that you can feed back to them in your suggestions – in essence they tell you what they need to hear to get better – and how to set up their unconscious to begin to notice their future in a way that means they've let go of their problem, i.e. they've achieved their solution state.

That whispering in my head to go and see Gil was one of the best things I've ever listened to. After the seminar I met Gil at his home and interviewed him for the *Hypnotherapy Journal*. He was pleased enough with the result that we began collaborating on his memoirs. For about a year I visited him and we talked about his life. Gil is a great raconteur and a fount of knowledge about the characters within hypnotherapy over the last fifty years, and I learnt so much from him. I was also using his videos to teach my students, so I had a great opportunity to do what NLP does – model excellence. One of the key things that kept popping up as I listened to him working with his clients was his use of C > E and A = B.

Now I have to make a distinction here. The pattern I am going to describe is a model based on what I observed in Gil's work, it's not a copy of the way he does it. When modelling something useful I first ask 'What are they doing that is working?' and then, 'Why is what they're doing working?' When I have a reasonable answer to those questions I've usually got something that I can teach to other people.

It's an approach that users of NLP have followed to capture excellence in others for many years now, but Gil was never comfortable with it, and on a number of occasions challenged me about it. I remember pointing out to him over lunch one day an occasion when I'd seen him, in my model of the world, anchor one of his clients.

He gave me a look that brooked no argument and said, 'I don't do NLP, I was around long before it was.' And of course he's right, NLP isn't a thing in itself, and it didn't invent anchoring. NLP provides a language to describe what people do so that they can do it better. The NLP steps to anchoring are just principles copied from people who were naturally good at it, that make it work well for most people most of the time. Gil may well have been one of those people. He certainly is now I've named an NLP pattern after him. But at the time I didn't argue, I just went back to eating my pie – if memory serves me correctly it was humble.

My point is that if we seek to simply imitate we don't evolve. What I hope this pattern does is take the essence of what makes it work so well with Gil and use its principles to further improve its range of use.

The Boynian pattern can be remembered by its ABC sequence and can be used firstly to identify the clients' evidence for their problem – their present state – and their evidence for their solution state – the future when they'd know they don't have their problem. Both begin at the same point, with a variation of the question format you learnt in Chapter 2.

Identifying their evidence for the problem state

When you launch into the Boynian pattern will vary from client to client. It may be appropriate in the first session, sometimes you won't have got them to this stage until later. It's also something you might use on several occasions. I hope that's vague enough guidance for you, now let's get on with it.

A The affirmation

Therapist: *In relation to your problem, if there was a something that you believed about yourself that is at the root of this problem, tell me what it is, beginning the sentence with 'I'.*
NB: Note the structure of that sentence.
Helen: I'm stuck and scared to move forward.

This affirmation provides the effect part (in the present) of the C>E equation. We want to know the deep structure behind it. So we move to the next question.

B Because (the cause)

Therapist: *Because?*
Helen: Because if I get things wrong people will think I'm stupid.

Sometimes a single question gets you to where problem-focused therapy would take hours to reach. Gil maintains that clients tell you all you need to know in the first five minutes. This is particularly true if you ask the right questions and have the ears to hear the answers. What that answer suggests is that the client has a history that has caused her mind to create a meaning pattern between what she does, and what people will think of her as a person. This is a classic mismatch that we learn when we're young. If you think of it in NLL terms, it is a confusion between what we do (behaviour), or what we're able to do (capabilities), and who we are (identity). How many times were you told as a child 'You're a bad boy (or girl)!' What was actually meant was, 'You've just *behaved* in a bad way.' Unfortunately aiming criticism at the level of identity sets up a belief that what we do and who we are are the same thing, so as adults we feel attacked if our idea is dismissed, or someone laughs at a mistake we make. We even make it in the way we describe ourselves. When meeting people for the first time do you say 'I'm a therapist'? What you mean is that you *do* therapy as your occupation.

The NLP trainers John Overdorf and Julie Silverthorn are fond of saying: 'Whatever you say you are, you're always more than that.'[5] And they're absolutely right. So whenever clients present themselves to you with a problem there is almost always (I really mean always, but I have a streak of caution in me) an algorithm at work that is basing their sense of self on the response of others towards their actions. This goes very deep. Some evolutionary psychologists suggest that the reason consciousness appeared was the importance of our place within the social hierarchy and that our sense of self is there to monitor our position within the tribe – our friendships, alliances, enemies, potential mates etc. The lower down we rank in the tribe the further from the carcass we sit, and the fewer opportunities we will have to pass on our DNA. It is an interesting idea that can be seen today in our consumer society – watch how advertising suggests a meaning pattern between what we own (that implies our capabilities to obtain it), what we do, and our status in society. Sad to think that we are the peak of evolution on this planet and so much of its inheritance is spent on assessing whether we're driving the right car.

The question 'Because?' might be followed by 'What else?' in order to reveal the full network of meaning patterns that underlie the original 'I' statement. Sometimes there will be several, other times just the one. Gil believes that the underlying neurosis present in all of us is 'I'm not loved or deserving of being loved.' While being very aware of Orr's Law in such circumstances, I have found this to be present in so many clients that I stand with him on it, and when a response to 'because' is along the lines of 'because they'll leave me/reject me/ not love me/like me' etc., then you know you're on the trail of a big one. The change you achieve with that client is likely to go far beyond her presenting issue.

When you have the response to B you move onto the third part of the pattern

C Complex equivalence – the effect (in the future) of the cause

Therapist: *And that means?*
Helen: That means I'll never fulfil my potential or do what I really want to do.

Let's again consider how wonderful we are. We are possibly the only species to consider consequences. No matter how often I say to my dog Barney 'Don't eat all that now, save some for later,' he doesn't – the brain of a walnut. The ability to predict the consequences of our present actions on our future is such a part of being human that we don't really consider the uniqueness of it, or the effect it has on our lives, but we're going to in detail later in the book. Returning to the earlier point about how much of our processing power is taken up with monitoring our social relationships, the ability to map cause and effect into the future gives a reason behind cooperation and even virtue. If I do something now how will it affect my safety and my place within my group later? Time will tell whether this is the true root of our ability to imagine the future, for now the fact remains that we have it and it is key to the success of therapy. Our mind is constantly working out the meaning of situations in our life based on our past experiences – we (mainly unconsciously) age regress all the time to accomplish this. And then the brain will compute the possible consequence to us of this situation in the future – it will positively hallucinate an age progression.

Steven Wolinsky in his seminal work *Trances People Live* suggests that regression and progression form the most common cluster of trance phenomena in a person's problem pattern, and the idea of the three algorithms tells us why this should be so. The past, present and future of our life is traversed constantly by our mind in search of the safest and longest route to our deathbed. It seeks patterns from the past to predict the route forward. Unfortunately for us, where the patterns of the past are based on negative premature evaluation, the future they predict is not going to be rosy. For example, a child has an SEE at the age of seven where she runs onto the stage as the star of the school play and falls head over heels to the uproarious entertainment of the crowd. If she evaluates that as embarrassment or humiliation then the unconscious will use that event to keep her away from any events that seem to be the same. So if, at the age of thirty her boss says, 'Helen, I want you to present to twenty prospective customers next Thursday,' Helen's mind essentially does the following:

1   It searches her memory for any SEE that is the same or similar to it (C > E or A = B).

2   It finds the memory string that began at seven (by thirty the string will have many other instances where performing in front of people = disaster).

3   Her mind age progresses to next Thursday and creates a positive hallucination of her talking to the group based on the experiences from

her past that have been selected. Not surprisingly it predicts her doing terribly. Now here's the rub; the body responds to images the mind creates (our imagination) just as strongly as it does to images that are formed in the mind as a result of information flowing through our senses – after all, the brain is using the same equipment for both functions. When we awake sweating from a dream with our heart hammering in our chest it's an example of the body being triggered into a response to the fevered imaginings of our dreams. So as Helen's mind's eye focuses on the forthcoming disaster her limbic system responds beautifully according to Freud's *Pleasure Principle*. It says: 'That doesn't look good, let's get ready to fight it or run away.' The flow of adrenalin is experienced by Helen as a queasy feeling in the stomach, by a sudden acceleration of her breathing and even sweaty palms. Classic fight or flight response. All Helen knows is that whenever she thinks of Thursday she feels – well, she might call it scared, nervous, frightened or anxious. That feeling grows stronger as Thursday approaches because the sabre-tooth tiger is getting closer and closer so more and more adrenalin is released. Perhaps on Thursday morning she'll be so paralysed by fear that she rings in sick. If she manages to make it to the presentation her expectation of how it's going to go will probably come true – what the thinker thinks the prover proves. Her emotional hijacking will take her into her 'performing = disaster' trance state and she may hallucinate the crowd looking unfriendly, feel all the unpleasant feelings we get when nervous, and of course strong emotions make us stupid so she'll fluff her lines and forget what she was going to say. Afterwards her unconscious appraises it based on her original SEE and says: 'Yep, we'll keep away from those in the future, I knew it would go badly.'

If suddenly presentations become a regular feature of her job she'll probably begin to look for something else, though she may come up with a number of reasons not connected to giving the presentations for her dissatisfaction with her job.

Our lives are subtly influenced by our unconscious guiding our choices according to the pleasure principle in this way. I recently moved house after living in the same place for twenty-four years. I really liked our new place, and yet as the big day came closer I found I was getting more and more emotional about it. On the day itself I felt completely emotionally hijacked all day. Okay, if you must know, at one point I sat in my shed and cried my eyes out – and I'm English for heaven's sake!

It was only later that I used self-hypnosis to figure out why. As a child I moved around a lot because my dad was in the RAF. Between the ages of five and eleven I attended nine schools. Each one involved being the new boy, making friends and then having to leave them behind. Without realising it my unconscious had come to a premature evaluation that moving equals loss. In my trance I remembered vividly standing outside Caterham Juniors waiting for my parents to pick me up to move to our new house. I was sobbing my heart out and one of my teachers stopped to try and console me. All I can remember is the sight of our shoes as I looked down ashamed of my tears.

'Dry your eyes at the back! And turn those violins off!' That's the trouble with a sequel: they always spend more on special effects. No wonder that, when my unconscious looked at the move and connected it with this string of memories, I experienced a fight-or-flight response at the prospect of moving – never mind that I was moving to a nicer house in a lovely spot. All my unconscious predicted as a result was loss. The fact that my adult children weren't moving with us compounded the situation beautifully. The real subtlety of the unconscious then began to dawn on me. Why hadn't I moved for twenty-four years? I had many rationalisations prepared – I wanted the children to have somewhere stable after my divorce, property developers were interested in buying it, it was convenient for work, etc. All of them valid in their own way. But I now believe it was just a simple complex equivalence that wanted to keep me stuck in a house in Slough, on a busy dual carriageway, next to a taxi business and a fire station, when the Cambridgeshire countryside beckoned – because to move equalled loss. And I'm damned if I'm moving again.

I hope this shows why knowing what the clients' unconscious predicts about the future, as a result of its perception of the problem pattern, is vital if we are to know what suggestions to make that will cause them to see their future more positively.

We find out by simply asking. Let's go back to the third part of the pattern.

> **Therapist:** *And that means?*
> **Helen:** That means I'll never fulfil my potential or do what I really want to do.

Helen's age progression is one that hallucinates her as unfulfilled or living a life she doesn't want – whatever that might be to her. So now we know the structure of the belief system pertaining to her problem across the three time frames of past, present and future:

> I'm stuck and scared to move forward because if I get things wrong people will think I'm stupid and that means I'll never fulfil my potential or do what I really want to do.

Not bad for defining their present state. It opens up a range of therapeutic directions, such as regressing to the cause of the fear of looking stupid, using the drop-through technique for that fear, or doing a parts integration.

I'll come to all of those in the book I'm not going to mention in this one.

Having defined the clients' belief system about themselves in relation to their problem, we can also use exactly the same patterns to get them to define their solution state – i.e., what would their belief need to be in the future for the problem to be resolved? What evidence would need to begin to flow through their senses for them to believe this is true?

Identifying their evidence for the solution state

A The affirmation

Therapist: *If you could make a statement that you'd like to be true in the future, which, if it was, would mean you'd be free of your problem, what would you say? Begin it with 'I'.*

Again note the presuppositional nature of the question.

Client: I am able to move forward and live the life I want.

B Because (the cause)

Therapist: Because?
Helen: Because I no longer need to be scared I won't live up to my mother's expectations.

C Complex equivalence – the effect (in the future) of the cause

Therapist: *And that means?*
Helen: *I can start to **live for myself**. I can do what is **important** to me and start **exploring** what's out there.*

I've highlighted the key words that the client uses to describe what she wants. I don't tend to include words that describe what she doesn't want, such as 'not being scared', because if I tell you not to think of a blue tree what happens? The mind can't process a negative so you have to think of the blue tree to not think of it. Similarly with Helen her mind has to fire the pattern that equals fear in response to the request not to think about it. This raises the chance of the fear coming back onto her radar into the future. Easier to follow the adage of 'think it how you want it'.

These words represent the evidence that, if the client were to start noticing them in her life, would mean that she's getting her outcome. I've noticed that replacing an old meaning pattern with a new one is much more powerful than simply negating the old one. Because the brain cannot help looking for consequences it makes sense to guide it towards the most positive consequence that the client can attach to your work. So, in any session, I suggest that you connect any technique you've used, or just the fact that you've had a session, with a future pace that creates a C > E or A = B relationship between it and the client's outcome. In its stripped-down version I mean a pattern that suggests the following:

> Because of X (what we've just done) you may begin to notice more of Y (evidence that equals the solution state).

Later I'll show you how to use this in a specific way in what I call the *change-link* pattern. The following is an example of a suggestion pattern that incorporates the words gleaned from Helen by the Boynian pattern into the Wordweaving™format, whereby suggestions have an aim, use trance phenomena to cause the shift in perception, and are linguistically framed to cause the client to create the full meaning for herself.

> ...and neither of us knows, yet, what will be the first thing you notice that lets you know you are *living for yourself*...how you begin to see the world around you differently as you start to *explore*...and it's not important yet whether you know what will be important *to you*...what it is that you begin to notice more and more around you that makes you realise that you are *living for yourself*...on your own terms...and you might be surprised at how you recognise strengths...and abilities within yourself...growing stronger with your belief that you can *explore what is out there*...to find what is important to you...so whether it is you or someone else who notices you're behaving differently...and it becomes so normal that you might forget these differences for longer and longer periods...because it is so much easier to focus on those things you discover around you as you *explore what is important to you about living for yourself*... etc.

If I break the pattern down into what it contains you can see what is layered into it:

(P = Presupposition   NLL = Neurological Level)
(TP = Trance Phenomenon   MM = Milton Model)

"....and neither of us know, *yet*,	yet = time (P)
what will be the *first* thing	first thing = ordinal (P)
you notice	notice = awareness (P)
that lets you know	that lets you = C > E (as you..then you..)
you are *living for yourself*	living for yourself = client's evidence
how you **begin**	begin = time (P)
to see the world around you **differently**	differently = algorithm A = not B sentence = positive hallucination (TP)
as you **start**	start = time (P)
to *explore*	explore = client's evidence
and it's **not important yet**	important = values (NLL) yet = time (P)
what it is that you	what = lack of referential index (MM)
begin to	begin = time (P)
notice, more and more	notice = awareness (P)
around you	around you = environment (NLL)

The Boynian Pattern

that **makes you**	makes you = C > E
realise	realise = awareness (P)
that you are **living for yourself**	living for yourself = client's evidence
on your own terms	
and you **might** be	might = modal operator of possibility (MM)
surprised	surprised = useful guiding state
at how you **recognise**	recognise = awareness (P)
strengths...and abilities within yourself	strengths/abilities = capabilities (NLL)
...growing stronger with your **belief**	belief = beliefs (NLL)
that you **can**	can = modal operator of possibility (MM)
explore what is out there	explore what is out there – client's evidence, also environment (NLL)
to find what is **important** to you	important = values (NLL)
so whether it is you **or** someone else	or = bind (MM)

who notices you're **behaving** differently	behaving = behaviour (NLL)
and it becomes so normal that you **might forget**	might forget = amnesia (TP)
these **differences** for	differences = algorithm A = not B
longer and longer periods	longer and longer periods = time distortion (TP)
because it is so	because = C > E
much easier to	much = adjective modifier (P)
focus on **those things**	those things = lack of referential index (MM)
you discover **around** you as you	around you = Environment (NLL)
explore what is important to you about living for **yourself**....	Identity (NLL) client's evidence

As you can see the pattern is framed in such a way as to include the client's description of her evidence 'explore what is important to you about living for yourself' etc., but it doesn't fall into the common trap of supplying **my** interpretation of what 'exploring what is important to you' would be to her, or what 'living for yourself' would be. If I had I would have found myself saying 'as you explore what is important to you, like...' or 'because you're living for yourself now you will...' In both of those examples I've begun to supply the new A = B (like) or C > E (because). That means we're now working from my model of the world instead of leaving the client's mind primed to notice anything that could fulfil her evidence criteria. Once you get the hang of this style of working life is a lot easier. The Boynian pattern gets you to ask the client what needs to happen in the future for her to know she's better, then all you have to do is create a suggestion pattern that primes her mind to anticipate it happening – what the thinker thinks will happen the prover proves will happen.

With the Boynian pattern to hand you might wonder what the need is for the questions we covered in the chapter on information gathering. Don't they achieve the same thing? Absolutely they do because they're using the same principles of similarity and causation. Both are presented within this book to give you flexibility and options. We don't live in an either/or universe – in reality, as you get used to this style of working, you'll flow between the two in response to the client's answers. I've separated them out to make their principles clearer, but it's important to realise that in a real therapeutic conversation there will be much more flow.

Chapter 4

Listening for trance

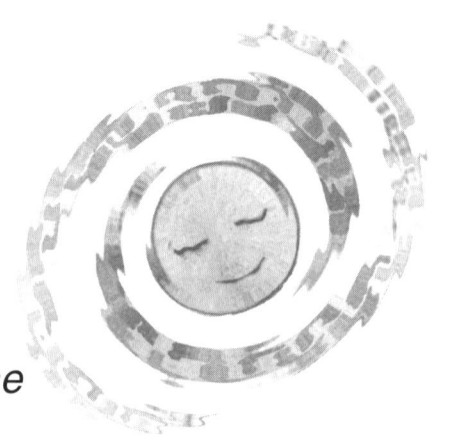

Trance is not a special state created by the hypnotist. There, I've said it. Depth of trance is not the major predictor of the effect of the suggestion you make – unless perhaps you make the same suggestion to everyone; deeper is not necessarily better. Trance is perfectly possible with eyes wide open – you've probably managed it loads of times when you've been bored in someone's company. All of the above fly in the face of many beliefs that traditional hypnotherapists adhere to, but fit comfortably within a modern view of trance that has evolved from several sources. Dave Elman and Gil Boyne both look upon trance as an agreement between therapist and client, something produced between them, not by one on the other. It is a firm move away from the Svengali-like model. Erickson, from an early stage, distanced himself from this way of thinking:

> The hypnotic state is essentially a psychological phenomenon, unrelated to physiological sleep, and dependent entirely upon full cooperation between hypnotist and subject.[6]

The modern view considers trance as part of everyday life, something all of us drift into unavoidably regularly – as much as ninety per cent of our actions may be driven by the unconscious. When you're driving home from work thinking about your day and suddenly realise you're home, who do you really think was driving?

The Milton and meta-models that were developed by Bandler and Grinder derive from what they termed 'universal modeling processes'; the means by which the unconscious reduces the background 2,000,000 bits of information the unconscious is aware of, down to the 7 plus or minus 2 bits the conscious can attend to – deletion, distortion and generalisation (see Volume I, p14). I suggest that the nine trance phenomena are the ways we experience these processes.

With deletion we're looking at the finite capacity we have for conscious awareness. We can pay attention only to so much, so anything we're not aware of is invisible to us. Much of what we pay attention to isn't actually by conscious choice – though it feels that way – but what is brought to the foreground because of unconscious calculations about its relevance or interest to us. 'Negative hallucination' involves the unconscious bringing to the foreground anything other than the object in question, like not noticing the spider you're scared of. In that way it's deleted from your attention. The same is true of amnesia, forgetting to think about the cigarette is usually achieved in a similar way to negative hallucination, by guiding the unconscious to make different choices about the information it brings to the foreground or leaves in the background. In a sense all the trance phenomena involve some degree of deletion, because if you're perceiving the world in one way you're not perceiving it in another – but I would mention just two more in particular: age progression and age regression. The former involves a single projection of your future (at a time), and so deletes all other possibilities – so seeing you make a fool of yourself doing the wedding speech leaves you quaking in terror because that's the only way you see it going, and age regression selects only those events from your past connected to your state of mind at that moment, because that's the memory string that's firing. Any memory that contains information contrary to the meaning of your present moment is deleted – so when you're remembering every time you've felt an idiot trying to get into conversation with someone you fancy, you overlook every memory of occasions when you've been a good conversationalist in a different context. It's another aspect of Orr's Law.

Distortion involves putting a particular spin on information received through any one of our senses. In an everyday scenario it's where we wave at a friend in the street and then realise it's not them and pretend we were only scratching our head. Our brain has mismatched the visual information, but in effect we've projected the likeness of our friend onto someone else. If we translate that into trance-phenomena-speak, that's what we refer to as a positive hallucination – distorting some aspect of what we see into something that isn't necessarily there. If you are nervous of public speaking then hallucinating the audience as interested and welcoming will do much to calm your nerves. Seeing a spider with qualities that prevent it being scary will also be helpful. The information we pay attention to from every other sense can also be distorted. We refer to this as sensory distortion. In everyday life you hear your partner say 'I didn't think you were going to wear that tonight,' and get upset because you distort that into 'Aren't you a bit fat to get away with that?' just because of his tone. That's an auditory distortion. Getting a cigarette to taste like the food you hate most is a gustatory distortion, and feeling full earlier in a meal would be a kinaesthetic distortion. In the sense that eighty per cent of the meaning of everything we experience is interpretation by the brain you could say that everything is some form of distortion – we know nothing as it actually is. Time distortion describes how our perception of time's passage varies according to the situation we spend it in, so we can make a visit by the in-laws go quickly, and the time since you've thought of having a cigarette seem ages. Dissociation is our ability to change our connection to ourselves or part of our body. Watching yourself giving birth from a distance helps you to control your experience of it. Letting your lips do your talking for you can change your perception of speaking enough to help you overcome stuttering.

Finally there is generalisation. This is the territory of the three algorithms of the mind and the rules the brain creates using them to calculate meaning and consequence. Many post-hypnotic suggestions are based on the principle of generalisation, anything the mind perceives to be different after a session with you could be viewed as the result of a post-hypnotic suggestion, whichever one of the trance phenomena you've employed to achieve it. Because of the way we connect memories together around context, and how our mind calculates consequence, the trance phenomena of age regression and age progression fall quite comfortably into this category.

I hope that's shown that there's a connection between NLP's 'universal modeling processes' and trance phenomena. To me they seem different ways of describing the same thing. The significance is that it shows trance states to be a prime factor in how our mind generates our reality, and so becomes a vital ingredient whenever we want to change the way we, or our clients, want to see the world. Within the model of Cognitive Hypnotherapy, trance phenomena become part of the *structure* of any pattern of information we perceive. That's what I meant when I said that trance is not a special state, it can be presupposed in just about any situation, but particularly a therapeutic one. Even resistance can be seen in terms of trance phenomena. If a client resists going into trance its because he's already in one.

From NLP has come a range of excellent techniques for adjusting clients' thought patterns, helping things from nail biting to curing a phobia in twenty minutes. Most of these techniques do not include a formal induction, and some do not even involve eye closure, but they are incredibly successful, and in my opinion part of their success lies in the fact that the technique itself – the mode of thinking that the client is led into – is trance inducing.

Steven Wolinsky has been the biggest influence in my philosophy about trance. He took it one step beyond its part in everyday life by realising that trance states – and the phenomena by which they are recognised – were absolutely central to the client's symptom formation. As I just said trance is a key part of the problem pattern – trance is how the mind 'runs' the problem. Do you panic when you see a spider? Why doesn't everyone else? Because your mind gets you to see the spider in a particular way – you hallucinate it in a dangerous form. How do people with anorexia manage to feel full after just three grapes? The mind creates that perception by distorting the feeling in their stomach. Wolinsky realised that people describe their problems in terms of the trance phenomena I've described. No longer can they be termed 'deep' trance phenomena, because deep levels of trance are not necessary for their appearance or use.

In Volume I, I described how trance phenomena could be utilised in your suggestions. I also laid down one of the rules of wordweaving: that every suggestion pattern should contain at least one trance phenomenon. After all, if trance phenomena are the way the mind runs the problem it makes sense that they are necessary to run the solution.

Given the choice available the inevitable question is: 'Which one do I use?' When I'm asked that by a student I invariably reply that in your early days just be grateful for any that come from your lips. However, with practice you will have a choice – and by listening to your client the 'right' choice will become apparent – because clients use trance phenomena to describe their problem. What I think you'll find is that clients tend to have individual preferences for which trance phenomena are used in their problem pattern – they're part of its structure. Again it makes sense to me that, like our senses, our minds will show a preference for some trance phenomena over others, and will use the ones it finds easiest wherever possible to achieve the effect it wants. So if you listen to a client and you notice she appears to use, for example, sensory distortion and negative hallucination most often in her description of her problem, then utilise these most often in your suggestions, because you know they're trance phenomena she can do – and if you've harnessed them as a focus for the client's solution state, then you've stopped them from being used to create her problem state at that moment.

If we go back to Helen and the information about her problem states that we obtained in the chapter on information gathering you'll remember we had the following:

- Certain types of people make her think they will find her stupid.
- These people tend to be people she is not close to or hasn't known for long.
- People in authority or in a position to judge her competence (i e stupid or not stupid) appear to be key.
- Any situation involving these people is anticipated as being scary.
- Helen knows she's in one of these situations because her mind goes blank, she feels sick and it's as if she's going to faint.
- Her face feels hot and her chest as if strapped with a tight band.
- The feeling in her chest feels 'fast'.
- If she imagines the next time she has to face a situation like this, the image is associated (through her own eyes), is close up and in colour.
- Her response to this feeling of fear is to flee.
- Afterwards she beats herself up about it.

If you need a prompt for the trance phenomena look in the Glossary. Can you identify the trance phenomena implied in Helen's description of her problem? Have a look for them yourself and then see if they match what's below. Just because they don't doesn't mean you're wrong, you may have picked up on something I missed.

- Certain types of people make her think they will find her stupid – likely to be a positive hallucination whereby Helen projects onto these people her feelings about herself.
- Any situation involving these people is anticipated as being scary – implies an age progression.
- Helen knows she's in one of these situations because her mind goes blank, she feels sick and it's as if she's going to faint – negative hallucination/amnesia (mind going blank) and sensory distortion.
- Her face feels hot and her chest as if strapped with a tight band. The feeling in her chest feels 'fast' – more sensory distortion.

From this we can be confident that if we use positive and negative hallucination, age progression and sensory distortion in our suggestion pattern then it's more likely that our suggestions will have an effect. These will be the trance states that create the perception of her solution state becoming true.

We now have everything we need to begin to create a suggestion pattern for Helen, so let's consider how to wrap up this first phase of therapy.

Chapter 5

The importance of the last ten minutes

By the end of the session you'll have obtained a lot of information – more than I have from Helen. It's quite common for the client to have had some level of revelation about his/her issue, or at least greater clarity. One of the most important factors in the eventual success of this relationship is for the client to realise – fully – that he/she is involved in the process of change. Many clients come with the attitude 'come on then, fix me' and expect to lie back and be made better. It suits the medical model and traditional approaches to hypnotherapy, but not Cognitive Hypnotherapy. Your greatest success will come with clients who take responsibility for their improvement, where they accept you as a tour guide, but not as a guru.

To that end I usually end the first session with a summary of what I've heard and where I think we should go. While I'm doing this with Helen I'm looking for signs of agreement; nods of the head, affirmative sounds. I'm also looking for frowns or any non-verbal indicators of disagreement. If the way I'm making sense of what she's said to me doesn't appear to meet with her agreement then I'll change the way I'm describing it until it does – her model of the world is the one we're working within, not mine. Within my explanation is emphasis on the 'we' aspect of the relationship, and how I'm helping her to change, not changing her. There's one other thing I look for this portion of the session to achieve – enthusing her.

I've found that the more successful I am in lending them my faith in their ability to change, the more likely they are to return for the next session, and the more they engage actively in their therapy. I've found that the graduates from my training programme who have the ability to pass their enthusiasm on to the client are the ones whose practices grow the fastest. In their book *Emotional Contagion* Elaine Hatfield, John Cacioppo and Richard Rapson look at how talking to depressed people tends to make *us* feel depressed, while being in the company of happy people makes us feel more buoyant. The authors propose that this emotional contagion occurs because we unconsciously synchronise with the facial expressions, voices, postures and movements of people we are communicating with. NLP has known of this for years and teaches techniques to utilise this phenomenon in order to establish rapport based on matching or mirroring the physiology, voice qualities and words of others. In *Emotional Contagion*, however, they suggest that some people are more contagious than others. The authors label them 'senders'. They hypothesise that senders probably possess at least three characteristics:

1. They must feel, or at least appear to feel, strong emotions.
2. They must be able to express (facially, vocally and/or posturally) those strong emotions.
3. They must be relatively insensitive and unresponsive to the feelings of those who are experiencing emotions different from their own.

I can see the rationale behind the first two conditions but would dispute the third. Just as there are senders there are likely to be receivers – so some people will be particularly aware of the emotions of the others.

But, receiving doesn't automatically mean responding. Some people will find it difficult not to get infected by the emotions they pick up from others, but others will have some form of resistance. Does the ability to send demand anything to do with the capacity to receive? It came to me that we could treat these characteristics as what are described as 'metaprograms' in NLP – programs that guide and direct other thought processes. In the words of Robert Dilts, metaprograms

> define common or typical strategies or thinking styles of a particular individual, group or culture.[7]

If being a *sender* is a metaprogram then it describes a continuum of potential. Some people will be excellent as *senders*, some will be poor, most will be somewhere between the two. Typically a distribution of this kind is represented as a bell curve as in diagram 5.1. High *senders* will be those people who naturally influence others by the 'force of their personality'. Conversely *not senders* will be people whose moods are hard to read, who will often feel misunderstood – the kind of people who light a room just by leaving it. What occurred to me was the possibility that the sensitivity to others' emotions could exist as a separate metaprogram. With the same bell-curve distribution

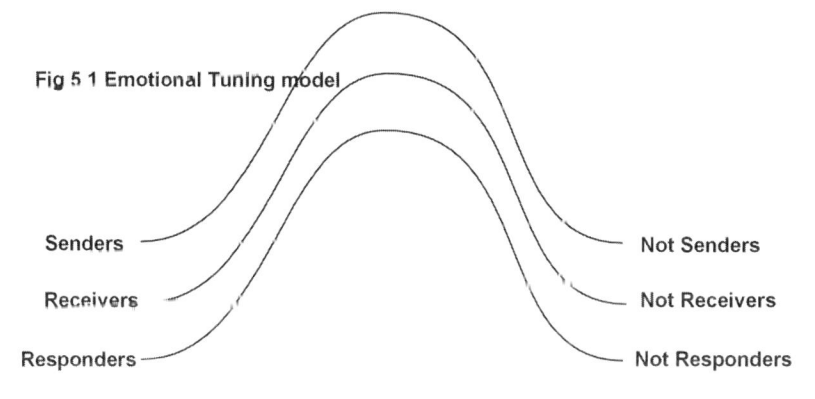

Fig 5 1 Emotional Tuning model

Senders — Not Senders
Receivers — Not Receivers
Responders — Not Responders

we'd have a range of people falling between two poles that I named *receivers* and *not receivers*. The former would be tuned to the emotions of others – in other words highly empathetic. At the other end of the scale would be *not receivers*, people who wouldn't be aware of the emotional signals people send – or not understand them if they were. Aspects of Asperger's syndrome may be described with this metaprogram. I was excited by this idea because it gave a combination of personality characteristics that could be used to predict areas of potential strength and weakness in my students and graduates. Clearly the most successful therapists are likely to be *high senders* (where the emotions they send are positive ones) and *high receivers*. They would be able both to tune into the emotions of their clients, and infect them with their own positive states. But it didn't feel complete. How come some receivers seem resilient in the face of a client's negative emotions, while others become infected? What explains emotional burnout in some of us but not others?

Recent research seems to indicate that our brains might be hard-wired in a particular way for empathising. UK researchers demonstrated that certain pain-processing regions of the brain light up when a loved-one is hurt. To hunt for this form of empathy, the researchers recruited sixteen heterosexual couples who were romantically involved and assumed to be attuned to each other's feelings. Each man and woman had electrodes, capable of delivering a mild, ticklish shock or a stinging, short jolt of pain, attached to the right hand.

Each woman then had her brain scanned by functional magnetic resonance imaging, while being able to view only the right hand of her partner sitting beside her. Unable to see her loved one's face, her only clue to his state was conveyed symbolically by a set of lights indicating whether he was receiving a mild shock or a stinging jolt.

When the women were subjected to a strong shock, a whole series of brain regions lit up including those on the brain's left side that physically mapped the pain to their hand. The regions of the brain – the anterior insula (AI) and the anterior cingulate cortex (ACC) – involved in the emotional response to pain and other situations, also lit up.

But when their partners were zapped, regions physically mapping the pain were quiet while the AI and ACC and a few other regions lit up in the women's brains. And the signals from those two areas were stronger in women who reported a greater degree of empathy, suggesting these regions mediate empathy.

So you don't actually 'feel' the physical pain – the partners didn't get a pain in their hand – but you 'suffer' with them. The researchers suggest that empathy is our brain running a virtual simulation that represents only the emotional part of the other person's experience.

Tania Singer, a neuroscientist at University College London who led the study said:

> That's probably why empathy doesn't feel like pain in your hand. It feels like when you anticipate your own pain. Your heart races, your emotions are engaged. It's like a smaller copy of the overall experience.

Singer suspects that our brain's ability to intuit the emotional response of others could have been strongly selected during evolution.

> If I do something, it tells me will it make you smash me, will you kill me or will you like it? Being able to predict how others feel might have been necessary for human survival....[8]

I would suggest that love is not a prerequisite for this phenomenon, just a connection between the two people that is strong and meaningful. A key feature of successful therapy has been proven over and over again to be the relationship forged between the people involved. Good therapists have the ability to create those kinds of bonds in their relationships with others, often without conscious effort. How ironic, then, that the very trait that disposes therapists towards effectiveness may also be the factor that leads to them becoming drained by their work. But it seems likely to me that this could be the basis for the high rate of burnout in our profession – because our brains simulate the experience of the client and we respond emotionally to their pain. Since the body cannot distinguish between real and imagined situations being processed in the brain we have a steady release of stress hormones throughout our working day preparing us to fight or run away. Over time this is going to lead to nervous exhaustion and even reactive depression.

Reading this research gave me a light-bulb moment. Our brains are predisposed to empathy, to understand the experience of another. But as with anything else, we're not all born equal. Some will be high responders – particularly susceptible to the emotions of others, and some will be immune. Just because we receive doesn't mean that we automatically respond. A computer might receive a virus, but if it has the right software it won't respond. So I sketched out a third bell curve – *responders* and *not responders*. *Responders* are those without anti-virus software who are most likely to get infected by the emotions flying around them, whereas *not responders* are those with the inoculations that make it possible to be discriminating about the moods they take on. So is there any way to protect ourselves from ourselves? I think there is. The great NLP trainer Tad James coined a phrase that I have heard myself repeating on many occasions to my own students:

> There is no content in content worth knowing.

Think about that. There is nothing about what happened to your clients that is important in itself, only the meaning they give it, so endless talking about their life serves no purpose. The more you learn to listen for the four categories of information (context, structure, process and consequence) present in every client's story (the content) the safer it will keep you from absorbing the client's pain.

In the light of this, in very general terms, because I don't like putting people in boxes, the metaprograms to aspire to in the context of therapy would be *sender, receiver* and *the lower end of the responder bell curve.*

Not sender and any combination of the other two could result in an otherwise excellent therapist who just doesn't pull in the clients.

Not receiver and any combination of the other two would probably be the kind of therapist who may be an excellent technician but lack the intuition to deal with what emerges in therapy, relying instead on fixed solutions, like reading the same script to clients with the same issue.

Responder and any combination of the two is likely to be the therapist who gets drawn into the emotions of the client and feel drained by his work. He's not likely to last in the profession without experiencing bouts of depression or anxiety.

In diagram 5.1 you could put a cross on the three bell curves as an honest estimation for where you feel you currently are. Make a copy and explain to your friends what the metaprograms are and ask them to put a cross where they think you are – the comparisons can sometimes be enlightening. If you think you need to work on becoming a better *sender* then you could study the techniques of rapport within NLP and recruit some friends to give you feedback about how they feel about what you're communicating to them (obviously don't pick friends who are *not receivers!*). Role-play situations where you look to convey enthusiasm or interest. Model those around you who seem good at it.

If you want to improve your skills as a *receiver* then the advice is similar to the above. Spend some time each day people-watching and look to interpret their moods. The book *Emotions Revealed* by Paul Ekman is excellent as a reference for what to look for and he also supplies software that trains you to recognise emotions in others more accurately.

Hopefully, if you know you tend to be a *responder*, following the practice laid out in this book of focusing on context, structure, process and consequence will assist you in upgrading your virus protection.

If you have all the clients you need, they regularly book further sessions (and turn up for them), recommend you to their friends, you look forward to work each day and leave the therapy room feeling good and with enough energy to continue the day, then you probably didn't need to read this section (*now* I tell you). If this is not the case think about these metaprograms and begin working on yourself. A good place to start is with the last ten minutes of the first session. Let them know you've been listening and have a good grasp of their issue. Put across your confidence that this understanding leads you to think you can help them and give them an idea of what you'll be doing with them next time. Give them any tasks you think helpful. When your rate of 'no-shows' declines and the recommendations go up you'll know you're making progress. Before you know it you'll be the Typhoid Mary of positive emotions.

Now, confident they'll return for the next phase of therapy, we can put the suggestion pattern together.

Part II

Creating and delivering the suggestion

**DELIVERY
Session Two:**

- Choose a technique to reframe the Context of their problem or change its Structure or interrupt its Process (or a combination of these)

- Use the information from session one to create a suggestion pattern that gets them to notice their problem state less and anticipate their desired state more.

Chapter 6

Creating the suggestion

We've worked through the first stage of developing suggestions. We're now at the point of designing the first suggestion pattern for Helen prior to delivering it. I've found with students that if they can begin a suggestion then their minds will generally finish it for them. I devised what I called a suggestion starter for them, which is replicated at the back of the book as Appendix 6. The idea is simply to take a phrase at random and add information from the client to it. The list of starters is by no means exhaustive and I exhort my students to extend their range by making up one of their own – it helps them to develop their own style – but for now the one provided serves to get you started.

People will go about developing their suggestions in different ways – some will just like to go with what comes, others like to build the script up using a framework. I'll walk you through a possible framework because it makes it easier to show what I'm doing, but discover what works for you.

Step 1

Take the client information and create suggestions aimed at moving him/her from the problem state to the solution state. Create three each for the NLLs of environment, behaviour and capability. Make one suggestion for values, beliefs and identity. This follows the first step of Wordweaving™

> Identify what aspect of the client's experience your suggestion is aimed at changing.

ENVIRONMENT

> And you might wonder how limitless the world around you seems now.
> We don't know yet what the first opportunity will be that you realise you can take.
> And many things in your life can begin to feel safe.

BEHAVIOUR

> So as you continue to find yourself breathing easily.
> And it may not be until afterwards, looking back, that you realise how easy you found speaking up.
> And more quickly than you might imagine you find yourself doing those things that get you noticed.

CAPABILITIES

> So whether it happens now or later doesn't matter, just that your confidence in the things you speak about is becoming strong enough for you to feel safe.
> After a while it just becomes normal that your determination is so strong that you feel free to assert yourself and speak freely.

It might be amusing just how surprised people are when you show them how quickly you pick something up and how competently you speak.

VALUES

Many things might begin to feel more important about enjoying the limitlessness of your potential.

BELIEFS

And it might not be until the third or fourth time it happens that you notice for the first time that you really are believing in yourself and can feel as good as anyone else.

IDENTITY

And we can both wonder when you'll look in the mirror and really believe you're worthy.

We can now use C>E and A=B to comply with the seventy/thirty rule to connect suggestions about environment, behaviour and capability with one about values, beliefs or identity. It would begin to look something like this:

And you might wonder how limitless the world around you seems now as you continue to find yourself breathing easily...so whether it happens now or later doesn't matter, just that your confidence in the things you speak about is becoming strong enough for you to feel safe **and that means** that many things might begin to feel more important about enjoying the limitlessness of your potential. We don't know yet what the first opportunity will be that you realise you can

CREATING THE SUGGESTION

take and it may not be until afterwards, looking back, that you realise how easy you found speaking up...but after a while it just becomes normal that your determination is so strong that you feel free to assert yourself and speak freely so that it might not be until the third or fourth time it happens that you notice for the first time **that you** really are believing in yourself and can feel as good as anyone else and that many things in your life can begin to feel safe...and more quickly than you might imagine you find yourself doing those things that get you noticed. It might be amusing just how surprised people are when you show them how quickly you pick something up and how competently you speak...**and that means** that we can both wonder when you you'll look in the mirror and really believe you're worthy.

Step 2

Some of the suggestion starters contain trance phenomena – 'and more quickly than you might imagine...' is a time distortion for example. But now we can go back and add some suggestions using the trance phenomena we noticed Helen using – negative and positive hallucination and sensory distortion (having noticed Helen's use of kinaesthetic predicates during her description of her problem pattern I would probably be putting particular emphasis on sensory distortion). This complies with the second step of Wordweaving™

> Choose which trance phenomena should be used to achieve that shift in perception in your client.

And you might wonder how limitless the world around you seems now as you continue to find yourself breathing easily...**so that as you're taking the opportunity to put your point of view you may not even notice how easily your knowledge flowed** so whether it happens now or later doesn't matter...just that your confidence in the things you speak about is becoming strong enough for you to feel safe and that means that many things might begin to feel more important about enjoying the limitlessness of your potential... . We don't know yet what the first opportunity will be that you realise you can take and it may not be until afterwards, looking back, that you realise how easy you found speaking up...and **how receptive the people listening were** but after a while it just becomes normal that your determination is so strong that you feel free to assert yourself and speak freely so that it might not be until the third or fourth time it happens that you notice for the first time that you really are believing in yourself and can feel as good as anyone else and that many things in your life can begin to feel safe...and more quickly than you might imagine you find yourself doing those things that get you noticed...it might be amusing just how surprised people are when you show them how quickly you pick something up and how competently you speak and **whoever it is you notice the most as you speak who makes you realise how competent you are just continues to help you feel those feelings of bubbly energy in the company of those people**...and that means that we can both wonder when you'll look in the mirror and really believe you're worthy.

Step 3

There are already a number of presuppositions and Milton model patterns present (it would be good practice to go through it and identify them), but we can read through it again and see if it would benefit by adding any further levels of subtlety. This is the third step of Wordweaving™ –

> Linguistically frame the suggestion to have the desired effect:

And you might wonder how limitless the world around you seems now as you continue to find yourself breathing easily...so that as you're taking the opportunity to **safely** put your point of view you may not even notice how easily your knowledge flowed so whether it happens now or later doesn't matter...just that your confidence in the things you speak about is becoming strong enough for you to feel safe and that means that many things might begin to feel more important about enjoying the limitlessness of your potential... . We don't know yet what the first opportunity will be that you realise you can take and it may not be until afterwards, looking back...that you realise how easy you found speaking up and how receptive the people listening were but after a while it just becomes normal **because** your determination is **becoming so strong** that you feel free to assert yourself and speak freely... . So that it might not be until the third or fourth time it happens that you notice for the first time that you really are believing in yourself and can feel as good as anyone else **so that** many things in your life can begin to feel safe...and more quickly than you might imagine you find yourself doing **well** those things that get you noticed... . It might be amusing just how surprised people are when you show them how quickly you pick something up and how competently you speak...and whoever it is you notice the most as you **do this** who makes you realise how competent you are just continues to help you **enjoy** those feelings of bubbly energy in the company of those people...and that means that we can both wonder when you'll look in the mirror **soon** and really believe you're worthy.

That's what I would describe as one suggestion loop, because it's a complete loop of all the NLLs. Clearly it hasn't utilised all the information gained from Helen so we could now continue and do as many loops as we need. To increase the length of the suggestion pattern to the twenty or twenty-five minutes that I think is optimum you could take each loop and rearrange the order of the suggestions within it so that a different set of environment, behaviour and capability suggestions is linked with a different one from values, beliefs and identity. It has the benefit of reinforcing the ideas by repetition and saves you having to come up with too many ideas. Obviously suggestions from different loops can be mixed and matched for the same purpose. The suggestions we put together from the Boynian pattern can also be integrated into the final version.

Bear in mind that what I've put together is just an example – it's not *the* thing to say after listening to Helen. You could take the information, follow the principles and come out with something different that would work just as well.

Session two: delivering the suggestion

Helen arrives for session two promptly, looking more relaxed this time but also nervous because she knows that now we're going to 'do something', not just talk. I have the suggestion pattern polished and ready. In truth it's almost certainly not the only thing I would do during this session; a technique aimed at changing her problem structure, interrupting her problem process or changing its context would form a significant part of the treatment plan (all of which will be in Volume III). However, after I've utilised whichever intervention I've felt suits the situation best, and with Helen relaxed, I'll deliver the suggestions to her, count her back out afterwards and then have a chat about her experience, taking the opportunity to throw in any useful post-hypnotic suggestions if the chance arises. I'm making the assumption that people reading this book will, in the main, be practising hypnotherapy already and don't need egg-sucking advice about inducing trance and the like. One thing to bear in mind, though, is the idea that people remain open to suggestions for a while after the 'proper' trance, so sometimes I'm still suggesting positive things as I'm showing them out the door! I'll take a note of anything Helen reports that strikes me as interesting or useful and then book the next appointment. One of my parting comments is usually something like, 'Most therapy happens between sessions, so just notice anything that's different or unusual for you.' It primes expectancy.

Part III

Gauging the differences that make the difference

> **CALIBRATION Session Three+:**
>
> - Calibrate whether the client perceives themselves to be improving.
>
> - If they do, use the Change-Link Pattern. Consider further interventions if appropriate.
>
> - If they don't then adjust the aim of your suggestions and continue using techniques to change the problem pattern. Continue until success is achieved.

Chapter 7

Calibrating and using change

In my early days – and I know a lot of my students do this – I'd prepare for this session and have a shopping list of what I was going to do next. However, what the client had to say about his/her experiences since the last session blew out my plans so often that I stopped planning and adopted the Fritz Perls' adage that Gil impressed on me: 'Deal with what emerges.' Spontaneity and flexibility are key attributes for the therapist to develop. Nowadays I wait for the client to tell me in what direction I need to go, so once Helen is settled in the chair and we've exchanged pleasantries I'll say,

> T: How have you been since I last saw you?
> H: Yes, good. I've had a good week.
> T: What have you noticed about yourself?
> H: Well, I've definitely felt a lot better. I actually stood up for myself in a meeting. I quite surprised myself!
> T: Brilliant! How did you feel as you were doing it?
> H: Fine, I just seemed to do it without thinking.
> T: And how did you feel afterwards?

> H: Yes, dead chuffed. Really pleased with myself I know it's only a little thing but it felt really good. I think my boss was pleased as well.
>
> T: So when you came to see me you said your self-confidence was about four out of ten in those situations. How is it now?
>
> H: Well, I'm still a bit shaky some of the time, but definitely better. Maybe seven?
>
> T: Seven? That's really good. If you were at a nine how would you know?
>
> H: How would I know? I'd be doing that kind of thing more often.
>
> T: Anything else?
>
> H: I know I'm not proactively looking to speak up. So if I was able to deliberately plan to present something – and do it – I'd really know I was getting somewhere.

I'm listening for anything in Helen's report that corresponds to the suggestions I made the previous week. For example, 'I think my boss was pleased as well' could be taken as a response to the suggestion 'and whoever it is you notice the most as you do this is who makes you realise how competent you are.' This reinforces my feeling that positive hallucination is a strong trance phenomenon to use with her and I'll make a mental note to use it again.

Helen's responses have also given me her evidence criteria for her next level of improvement – doing more presentations – so we need to incorporate her evidence into our suggestions for this session. It's not going to be possible to wait a week while you write it out so I've put a pattern together within which you can slot this information until you're ready to ad lib. I call it the change-link pattern because it focuses on the things that have occurred since the last time I saw the client that have enabled the improvement he/she reported. It then links these changes to the anticipation of further improvement in the future.

Ah, I hear some of you say, what happens if the client comes back and says that there's been no improvement? First I remember that wonderful NLP presupposition, 'There's no failure, only feedback.' Whatever the client reports back with remains just information. If there's no improvement either I haven't tapped in the right place or I haven't tapped for long enough. In most cases I'd continue with regression or whatever other techniques seem appropriate and repeat the original suggestion pattern – or a variation of it if I need to incorporate anything Helen's volunteered in session three that I think is relevant.

The following pattern works by taking any and every change that has created a perception of improvement in the client and linking them together to form the basis of future expectation in the client. I use it each and every time a client returns and reports positive change, usually towards the end of a session when the client is comfortably in trance:

Change-link pattern

And just imagine floating back along your past...all the way back to the last time I saw you...and it doesn't matter if you don't yet know...or if you never know...what it was exactly that made the difference...for your unconscious mind to assist you in the changes you've been noticing...and it can be interesting that for you to have noticed the positive things that have been happening...something about you must have changed...the way you're thinking

...feeling...and often these changes are happening so unconsciously that we're not even aware of them as they're happening...so if I were to ask your unconscious mind instead to take all the time in the world to come back towards now...noticing all the differences in you that have made this possible...the way you're behaving...the differences in the way you're responding to people around you...how they're responding to you positively...those things about you that are growing stronger...helping you in the most powerful and positive ways.... So whether there's something yet you can believe as a result of how you're noticing being different that could help this continue and develop and grow even stronger, which means whatever it needs to mean for this change to be lasting...to be able to follow these improvements...and changes in you all the way back to now...and just imagine how...if your unconscious were to use these changes as a platform for your future...how that future could begin to appear in front of you...just as you want it...with all the things that are important to you...present...and just enjoy being aware of all of the things in this new future...all the things that can help you to move towards them...to continue to motivate you to move towards this new you...doing everything you need to do to bring this future towards you as quickly as it's possible...so just put that image of your new future wherever in your future seems right so your unconscious can help you move towards it in the way it supports you...assisting you in doing all

> the things that bring it closer...and come back to now when that's done...and open your eyes after I count to five....

This also works very well in tandem with an arm-drop. As you get to the part where you say

> so if I were to ask your unconscious mind instead to take all the time in the world to come back towards now...noticing all the differences in you that have made this possible...

take one of your client's arms by the wrist (with permission) and raise it to about shoulder height. Then say something like,

> as your hand gently returns to your lap, only as quickly as your unconscious mind can notice and store these differences...slowly sinking down as your unconscious mind is noticing... [and returning to the script] the way you're behaving...the differences in the way you're responding to people around you...etc.

Pace the rest of the suggestion pattern to the speed of the client's hand and extemporise using any information you gained about the client's solution state during the original information gathering, or from that of your current session. In Helen's case, from session three, I could incorporate within the change-link pattern:

> ...and it might surprise us how soon you find yourself speaking up comfortably again. And whether you realise you're about to do it or it's

only afterwards, looking back, that you realise how spontaneously it happened doesn't matter...just that the way you see that environment now as being one you belong in...comfortable and safe because you are worthy means that it's natural for you to look for more and more opportunities to assert yourself...and the more you look the more you see...around you so many good opportunities just right for you....

Be aware that problem patterns often exist in relation to others, so as they feel the relief from their immediate issue something else bubbles up. A person's anger problem might mask something they're scared of, so as they let go of their stuff (technical term) about anger they start talking about fear. You focus on resolving that and then wait for anything else to surface. It's one of the reasons why change tends to be discontinuous – it sometimes feels as if you help the client take three steps forward only for them to report the next week that they've staggered two steps back.

Clients and new therapists tend to expect that the effect from therapy will be something like Figure 7.1, a smooth and steady feeling of improvement. This can happen, but more commonly what is experienced is something like Figure 7.2.

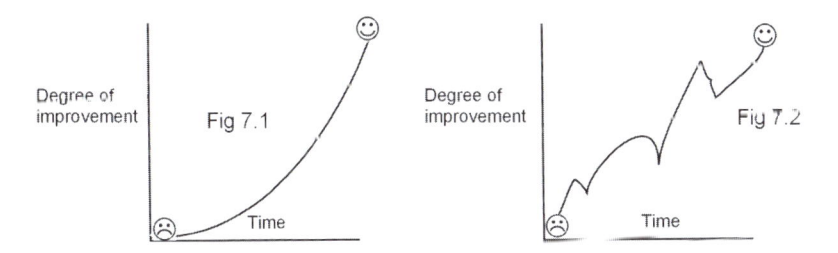

Fig 7.1 — Degree of improvement vs Time

Fig 7.2 — Degree of improvement vs Time

I've come to realise that it's just a normal part of the process but it's why it's important to keep the client's focus on the solution state by calibrating how much better he/she currently is compared to the original problem state. After a few sessions, even if the client had a setback week he/she will still be aware of the overall trend if you place their attention on it.

Another thing to calibrate each session is the current energy of the client. If you did a major intervention the previous week then he/she may not feel ready to do anything significant in the next, so a simple relaxing trance induction and some suggestions in the vein of the change-link pattern might be all you do. Sometimes you won't even do that, the client will just want to talk. This is neither wasted time nor an absence of value, so long as it's viewed as a pause at the bottom of one slope on the graph in preparation for the next ascent. If you notice a pattern emerging where the client is wanting to 'chat' more than to work then it might be an indication of unconscious resistance – there's a knowledge of something waiting to emerge that the unconscious thinks is better kept where it is. This is where rapport and good questioning help to keep the client focused on what he/she came to see you for. Resistance is just information and we return to a variation of an earlier question, 'What do I need to know about this resistance that will mean I can help the client resolve it?' It just becomes another part of the puzzle that keeps therapy one of the most fascinating occupations you can find.

As you continue calibrating the client's shift towards the solution state the new layers will diminish, any resistance you meet you'll resolve, and the momentum of change seems good. As this happens your sessions will increasingly shift from focusing on reframing the client's past (because that job will be done), or disrupting the client's problem pattern (because it will have ceased firing significantly), and begin to concentrate instead on re-tuning the client's anticipation and experience of a positive future. Much of the rest of the book is devoted to why it's so important and how we can accomplish this.

Part IV

The last piece of the jigsaw

> **CONSEQUENCE Session Four+:**
>
> - Once client is experiencing positive change include visualisations to prime the mind for positive expectancy (Rocking Chair and Luck Scripts).
>
> - End therapy when client considers themselves to have achieved their goal(s) and progress appears ongoing and self-sustaining.

Chapter 8

The importance of consequence

"In many ways intelligence is really a measure of our capacity for prediction."

Steven Johnson

Buddhism exhorts us to 'be in the now', to **be**...**here**...**now**. Try it. Just for a few minutes, but without closing your eyes or going into any kind of meditative state, focus on what is around you, what is available to your senses. Come back to me when you've done that.

How did that go? Personally I find it impossible to maintain my focus on the moment for any length of time. Within moments my mind drifts somewhere else. Oh well, nirvana no time soon, and it's not surprising. We feel as if we are moving through distinct elements of time and space – seconds, minutes, hours, days, etc. We have a sense of life being solid and real as we travel in time through it, but the moment *now* is just the physical interface between the world and the fabric of the mind – and that point of contact is like the tip of the iceberg; the information each moment of now contains is only a fraction of the universe our mind creates at the same moment. Mainly out of our awareness our mind lives in a world that simultaneously contains all of our past, now, and the future it anticipates. Like an ant in the Eden Project we tend to mistake where we are for where there is, and only dimly see the extended matrix surrounding us – the big picture.

We're sitting in a physical universe, aware of only a tiny proportion of it – but all of it exists all of the time. We're also sitting in a mental universe, aware of only a tiny proportion of it – but all that has happened in our life, and all the possibilities that the mind calculates could happen, exist in our mind at every moment. Adjusting any part of this mental universe will affect all the other parts, and our perception of the physical universe it connects to.

So if we live in this mass of connections between our past, the present we interpret as a result of it, and the future we calculate as a result of it, then it follows that our therapy should

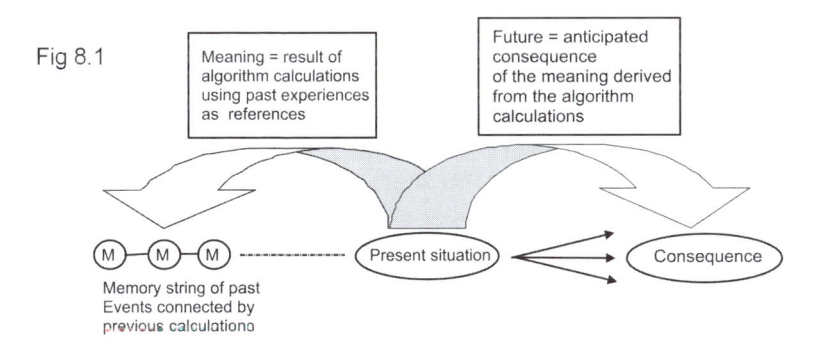

Fig 8.1

Meaning = result of algorithm calculations using past experiences as references

Future = anticipated consequence of the meaning derived from the algorithm calculations

(M)–(M)–(M) ---------- (Present situation) ⟶ Consequence

Memory string of past Events connected by previous calculations

acknowledge this. Even further, it should utilise it. Every session, every intervention, should form the basis of an improvement in the client's anticipation of his or her future.

The future doesn't exist yet, but how we imagine it determines whether we look forward to it – and feel motivated about moving towards it – or whether we dread it and find our unconscious doing everything it can to keep us where we are. Even though we don't like where we are. So as therapy progresses it is vital to prime the client to anticipate an improvement in response to the session you've had with him or her, and as the therapy progresses to link the positive differences he/she is noticing to an anticipation of continued positive change. Over time, and usually not that long a time, the client's unconscious begins to produce age progressions that are positive. This will create in the client more energy, more optimism, new beliefs about him or herself, and even begin to change his/her version of history. Because that's how memory works. Our history is a fabrication, and we have no real way of checking its veracity. Of course you can ask your brother if he remembers pushing you out of the tree, and if he does he probably did, but you can't ask anybody if that really caused you to feel you couldn't trust men. Your beliefs are created in response to your exposure to information (and experiences equal information), but once these beliefs have been formed they become the lens through which you recall your memories. Once again Orr's Law raises its head. If you have a belief that men can't be trusted, when you think of your past the events in it will be interpreted by the prover to verify the belief the thinker holds. The more unhappy we feel about our life, the more we'll remember our life being unhappy, which then creates the anticipation of more unhappiness, which then primes us to notice only those things that create our unhappiness. It's a very nasty vicious circle that needs to be broken. And your work needs to focus on breaking it in every time frame, past, present and future.

Because of this the sessions subsequent to those described continue in the same vein: tapping away with your techniques to change or disrupt any patterns created by poor past programming and supporting the effects you get from the techniques by sensitising your clients to changes in what they notice about the present that they link to your work, then connecting them through your suggestions to the anticipation of further improvement.

We ended Part III at the point where new aspects of the client's issue stop emerging, and overall the client perceives a sustained progression towards his or her outcome. It's at this time we focus on further tuning his or her mind to anticipate a future happiness. The field of Positive Psychology is demonstrating the value of optimism for creating health and well-being and increasingly I work to improve the ability of the client to be positive about his or her future. I hope I've already convinced you of the importance of how we imagine our future – and that our mind constantly attempts to calculate the consequences to us of the situations we find ourselves in and the actions we take. A relatively new theory has raised awareness of our minds' use of consequence that we might need to take into consideration when we use age progression to help the client imagine a better future.

Although the ability to imagine has been a major factor in our success as a species, it has also brought with it a downside – being able to think of the future brings with it the knowledge of our own mortality. Surely knowing we're going to die must have some effect on us? In the words of Tom Pyszczynski, Professor of Psychology at Colorado Springs,

> What an appalling affront to share the intense desire for continued existence with all living things but be smart enough to recognize the ultimate futility of this most basic biological imperative....[9]

Yet it's odd, isn't it, that we know we're going to die and yet most of us don't yet appear to get anxious about the prospect. You'd think we'd live in a constant state of fear. Indeed, surely it would give us a real perspective on everyday concerns? I've often found it strange how people worry about things that in the light of our mortality become trivial. If it's not something you're going to worry about on your deathbed why get in a state about it now? I think embracing the knowledge that we're all going to die (how come the law of averages doesn't apply with death?) can bring a wonderful freedom. One day I'm going to be dust – so what am I going to do with the time I have before that happens? And because we all end up at the same finish line, whatever course we choose to run, what can really go wrong? However, I know that's not a view shared by everyone, and a new field of study suggests that unconsciously the knowledge of our death does have a profound effect on how we conduct our lives, and that some elements of our personality – like belief systems – have evolved as a coping strategy. This area of psychology is called Terror Management Theory (TMT), with Pyszczynski being the leading voice. He argues that death-defying activities such as parachute jumping and climbing are forms of repression and denial (and not dissimilar to the therapeutic paradox – see Appendix 1), and that the way we construct our societies, the way we see ourselves and the way we treat others, is the result of evolved mechanisms that act to repress our fear of death. Our 'life' might be something we immerse ourselves in just to distract us from thoughts of our death.

The interest of Pyszczynski and two of his friends, Sheldon Solomon and Jeff Greenberg, was originally piqued by reading the work of Ernest Becker, who won the Pulitzer Prize in 1974 with his book *Denial of Death*. He argued that we bolster our self-esteem by defending ourselves against personal attacks, and invest so much importance in our belief systems because they and our sense of self are buffers between us and the fear of oblivion that we all hold. The three friends decided to find out if he was onto something and developed a series of clever experiments to test Becker's hypothesis. The first was designed to test how being aware of our mortality affects subsequent behaviour towards someone who violates an aspect of our belief system. They asked a group of judges to write a few sentences about what they thought would happen to them when they died, and how this made them feel. They were then given a hypothetical case of a woman accused of prostitution and asked to set a price for her bail. A control group of judges was given the same task without having been primed to think about their death beforehand. The average bail set by the first group was $455, while the control group asked for just $50. So much for Justice wearing a blindfold.

The second experiment sought to investigate the connection between fear of death and self-esteem. They divided volunteers into two groups and gave them bogus feedback about a personality test they took as part of the experiment. The first group was given positive feedback, the second group less glowing. Half of each group was then shown film clips showing images of death, while the other half viewed neutral footage. When the researchers tested anxiety levels by asking subjects how they felt, they found that those who'd had their self-esteem boosted beforehand were able to watch the death-related footage without feeling any more anxious than those watching the neutral footage. Without the boost the death-related images aroused considerably more anxiety than the neutral ones. What does this show us about the purpose of self-esteem? According to Greenberg,

> [it's] convincing us that we are significant beings. By being more than just animals we persuade ourselves that we are not subject to the natural laws of decay and death.[10]

Solomon, Pyszczynski and Greenberg were convinced by the results of such experiments that imagining the universe to be a place of meaning and order helps us cope with the terror of death. Concepts such as the soul and the afterlife – or reincarnation – offer us the prospect of immortality. Symbolically we achieve immortality through our connection to family, nations, and causes – things that are more enduring than ourselves – and through tangible reflections of our existence, such as children, money or culturally valued achievements; such reflections could range from Alexander conquering most of the known world by the age of thirty-two, to Joe Bloggs buying a new car. This is a recursive loop because by investing in the symbolism of a world view, we also become invested in living up to it. We sign up to a culture in order to bolster our self-esteem, but then have to work to measure up within that culture in order to achieve that boost. Anybody spot the seeds of our current angst, anxiety and lack of fulfilment in our modern, consumer-driven world?

Although these ideas met with scepticism when they were first published in 1985, more than 200 studies have been carried out since suggesting that we respond to reminders of our death in predictable ways. In one study Greenberg found that people valued charity more highly if they were interviewed next to a funeral home than elsewhere on the street. In another, the researchers presented US subjects with two problems that could best be solved in the first case by sifting black dye through the US flag and in the second by hammering a nail with a crucifix. People forced to contemplate their death took much longer to solve the problems and Solomon, Pyszczynski and Greenberg believe that this is because death thoughts made people uneasy about using these US and Christian icons in inappropriate ways.

Other studies have shown that reminders of death have the effect of making people strive to bolster their self-esteem: people who prided themselves on being good drivers tended to drive more boldly and those who valued their appearance focused on improving it. The experimental evidence leaves little doubt that we are affected by our own mortality and that good self-esteem is a vital factor in our well-being. That last bit of information isn't new, but TMT suggests a new reason why this is so.

One last thing before we make this relevant to therapy. A Dutch social psychologist called Dijksterhuis primed his subjects along certain themes. In one instance he primed volunteers to think about old people. Amazingly he found that when you are primed like this you actually take on the characteristics of elderly people, at least temporarily. This particular group was given a memory test after priming and performed significantly less well than a control group. Even more striking was the finding that if you're primed to think about stereotypically stupid people – football hooligans, soap stars – your performance in a subsequent IQ test will drop. In short, thinking about stupid people makes you stupid. If you needed a reason not to watch *Big Brother* this is it. What do we take from this? That **we become what we think about.**

How can we use this usefully in therapy? Let's connect what we've covered so far:

> We live within a reality bubble that is created by the calculations of our unconscious mind.

> This reality bubble includes our complete interpretation of our past, and the awareness of our calculated future up to and including our death.

> How we imagine our future affects our actions in the present. The pleasure principle suggests that we'll be motivated towards what we calculate will bring us pleasure, and seek to avoid what will bring us pain. To that end we feel anxious as a result of negative images we create of our future.

> Often these images are unconscious, so we feel anxious without realising why.

> TMT suggests that the basis for self-esteem is as a means of reducing our fear of death. We construct belief systems through which our sense of self is boosted.

> The more clearly we feel we are living a fulfilled life the better will be our sense of self-esteem.

Now let's take it one step further. **If we think of ourselves in a certain way we are likely to become that way**, so the more we tune the mind to imagining us having all the attributes of who we'd be if we were who we want to be, the more we'll become that person.

How about if we already believed we were going to die totally fulfilled? How much more likely would it be that we'd make the life choices that would lead us to becoming the person who achieves that level of fulfilment?

I suggest that what we need to do, for both ourselves and our clients, is to prime our mind with positive expectations. First let me give you a visualisation exercise that creates a potential future that leads to a sense of fulfilment. It fulfils the predictions of TMT and utilises what Dijksterhuis postulates.

The Rocking-Chair exercise

First induce trance:

...and from here if you could go out to the end of your long and fulfilled life...all the way to that moment where you could look back from your rocking chair...satisfied with your life and what you achieved...what you experienced ...for your unconscious to become fully aware of the person you are in the future...the person you became from your long and fulfilled life...the best possible you...the you you'd be happiest being...now...for you now to be able to feel that sense of fulfilment and satisfaction at the life you've lived...and the person you are...the way you think...what you believe...those things that are important to you...and as I raise your arm just allow it to slowly return to your lap only as quickly as your unconscious can absorb all of the things that make you so content with your life...spending all the time you need to absorb all of your qualities...to really get a feeling or a sense for this...so that your unconscious mind could bring all of these things back with you...and becoming aware as you come back to now of the choices that you made in your life that led you to becoming this you in the future...all that you did to live your life the way you'd most want...to become the fulfilled you in the rocking chair...all the time in the world to absorb the subtle directions your life can be guided to in the future so that from today your unconscious can be aware of this rocking-chair moment ahead of you ...helping you choose those directions and decisions that take you towards that fulfilment ...and how good it can be to begin to feel this movement towards that goal...knowing it's out there...guiding you towards your best life choices...giving your unconscious the time it needs to begin this process as I count from one to five....

As with the change-link pattern, pacing your suggestions is very important here, you must leave the client time to respond to them. You can even set up an ideo-motor signal to let you know when the unconscious has finished processing each part of the suggestion pattern. Let them take their time and they can often have a really profound experience. As someone who has benefited greatly from having the 'fulfilled me' ahead of me in my future, I really can feel the gentle tug as my unconscious guides me in the decisions I make. It's like a conscience that doesn't use guilt to get you to do the best thing.

This is one pattern that you can begin to use on the client, probably from session four. It can be repeated to consolidate the new pattern in the brain that it represents. If your clients begin to see the decisions they make being based on whether it takes them towards or away from the fulfilment they see for themselves in the future, it becomes a potent force for positive change. Their rocking-chair image needs to be clearly ahead of them, so reinforcement of it is important. If we can also generally make our clients more optimistic and more motivated to take action to achieve their goals then their improvement is likely to be even swifter.

Some other recent research suggests what we need to do to achieve this.

Chapter 9

Think yourself lucky

The Boynian pattern, when used to identify the solution evidence, moves our clients' attention to an anticipation of a positive future. As I've already suggested, this focus on creating a positive age progression is critical to successful therapy. When people say, 'I'm looking forward to the future,' they are being more literal than you might at first imagine. What they are telling you is that they have an internal representation (a thought made up of visual, auditory and/or kinaesthetic qualities – and maybe even olfactory and gustatory) of a future that is positive. Similarly if someone says, 'I have nothing to look forward to,' it communicates one of two things: either they have no internal representation of their future, positive or negative, or the future they do imagine has nothing positive about it. But so what? The future hasn't happened yet, and we don't create it, so why should it matter how we think about it? Because in many ways we do create it.

In the last chapter I mentioned the word priming and gave several examples of experiments that utilised it. In psychology the term priming refers to an increase in the speed or accuracy of a decision that occurs as a consequence of a prior exposure to some of the information in the decision's context. In other words, exposure to information will bias what we notice that is contextual to that information after that exposure. So if you're trying for a baby all of a sudden everyone around you seems to be pregnant. Priming is a consequence of the pattern-hunting that Kurzweil describes. The brain is excellent at seeing what it expects to see. As the British scientist John Lubbock once remarked, 'What we see depends mainly on what we look for.'

In an experiment that has become a classic of its time the Harvard psychologist Daniel Simons had volunteers watch a thirty-second clip of film where six people are playing basketball. Three were wearing white T-shirts and three were wearing black T-shirts. The observers were asked to count the number of times the people in white T-shirts passed the ball to one another. At the end of the film they were asked if they spotted anything unusual. Most didn't. When they were shown the film again they were amazed to see a person in a gorilla suit walk among the players, beat his chest to the camera and walk off. Interestingly if people are asked to watch how many times the players in black T-shirts pass the ball to each other they are twice as likely to spot the gorilla – the brain likes things that are similar.[11] The more things are different from what is expected the less likely the brain is to bring them to the foreground. **The more the brain is led to expect to notice something the more likely it is that it will.** This is true of your clients. If they are looking forward to their future their mind is primed to notice the possibilities that will manifest it. If they are expecting that nothing good will happen then they are less likely to notice the positive opportunities that occur in their day. As Winston Churchill said: 'An optimist is someone who sees opportunity in every disaster. A pessimist is someone who sees disaster in every opportunity.' Connect that to the view of the poet Ralph Waldo Emerson, who said that 'People only see what they're prepared to see,' and you have the pattern that presents in most clients.

If their brain has been tuned by its experiences to expect things to go well then things on a different frequency won't tend to be picked up. Conversely, if it's been led to believe that things will turn out badly, then anything that suggests the contrary will be distorted or deleted. How many times does 'What the thinker thinks...' show up?

So an integral part of therapy becomes retuning the brain to pick up different information from the environment – specific information that by its being noticed presupposes a shift in the clients' belief system. Having made the point that this information is best provided from the clients' model of the world, are there specific things to get them to focus on? Funny you should ask, yes there are.

Professor Richard Wiseman has done us a profound service through his curiosity about luck; he studied the differences between people who consider themselves lucky and those who don't. His research showed that fifty per cent of us consider ourselves consistently lucky, while fourteen per cent think of ourselves as consistently unlucky. Interestingly people tend to report that luck, or a lack of it, is cross-contextual – if they're lucky in business they find they're also lucky in love, while people who get a 'Dear John' text on the way to work find the car they've crashed into from the shock turns out to have their boss sitting in it.

Professor Wiseman was the right man to be studying this area. He came to psychology from an unusual background – that of stage magic. Being a master of illusion and distraction he became fascinated by the psychological principles that underlay his work. Not surprisingly, when he established a research unit at Hertfordshire University, his interests turned to investigating mediums, healers and psychic detectives. Eventually Lady Luck reared her head. He quickly realised that being lucky could not be a matter of chance – it was too consistent a factor – something had to be causing it. But what?

In his eye-opening book *The Luck Factor* Wiseman identifies four psychological characteristics shared by lucky people.

1. Lucky people create, notice and act upon the chance opportunities in their life.
2. Lucky people make successful decisions by using their intuition and gut feelings.
3. Lucky people's expectations about the future help them fulfil their dreams and ambitions.
4. Lucky people are able to transform their bad luck into good fortune.

He includes twelve sub-categories drawn from the four key principles. Taken together they provide a model for creating luck in your life. For our purposes they are a wonderful guide to what we should be priming the clients' mind to anticipate in order for them to create their life in a more positive way. After all each of us is surrounded by opportunity and possibility every day, but whether we notice them or do anything about them depends on what our unconscious brings to the foreground and then what it calculates is in our best interest to do about it. What does this sentence say?

Opportunityisnowhere

There are two interpretations of it. Did you notice both or just one? If both, which one came to mind first? The meaning your unconscious took from it would be a factor in your response to it, don't you think? If you believe that opportunity hangs around you like an orchard then your mind is primed to pick the fruit, but if you think you live in a desert you'll be primed to notice the sand in your shoe. Wiseman set up an interview in a coffee shop with two volunteers, one who thought of himself as lucky, the other not. They were asked to arrive at different times and the situation was rigged with two different opportunities for good luck. First, a five-pound note was placed on the ground outside the coffee-shop door. Martin, the lucky one, picked his up, Brenda, the unlucky one, stepped right over it. Once inside they both found just one available seat next to a stooge, who happened to be a successful businessman. Within minutes Martin had struck up a conversation with him. When it was Brenda's turn she sat beside the businessman but said nothing.

Later when Wiseman turned up to interview them he asked them if anything lucky or unlucky had happened to them that day. Brenda looked blankly and reported an uneventful morning. Martin, on the other hand, launched into his good fortune at finding the fiver and the interesting chat he had. As Wiseman remarks: 'Same opportunities. Different lives.'[12]

Wiseman's first principle gives us three time-based steps through which we can explore his discoveries and incorporate them into Wordweaving™.

Lucky people **create**, **notice** and **act** upon the chance opportunities in their life.

Create chance opportunities.

Most luck doesn't happen in a vacuum. Certainly a hermit is capable of winning the lottery, but most of the things that people value – and which they measure their luck through – involves their place within society. Polls consistently show that good relationships are the key to a sense of well-being, and in a society that seems to create a sense of isolation for those within it those who feel luckiest are in supportive relationships with friends, family and partners. I have had so many clients suffering from feeling unloved and in despair of meeting the 'right' person. Yet when I ask them, 'What are you doing to meet this person?' overwhelmingly they admit to not doing much. They hope that somehow love will come to them, usually while they're sitting watching a romantic movie in their living room. No offence, but the chances of it actually being the pizza delivery man are pretty slim. Lucky people create opportunities for themselves, by investing energy in building and maintaining social networks, by being open to new experiences and believing that their interactions with people are likely to be productive and successful.

Notice chance opportunities.

Lucky people tend to be more relaxed about life and are guided by their gut instincts. They expect any good luck to continue, and when things go wrong they don't dwell on it, or connect it to past mistakes. Lucky people are able to see the silver lining, the opportunity in every disaster.

Act upon chance opportunities.

Everything that has ever been achieved that's worthwhile began with a dream. Success requires having a dream and then acting upon it. I spent a lot of years waiting for my life to change for the better before I woke up and got the message that you have to make life happen. 'Take action' has been my mantra ever since. Lucky people attempt to achieve their goals, even when chances for success appear slim. They expect that any ill fortune will ultimately turn out to be for the best.

So if this is the recipe for bringing luck into the life of our clients, how do we get them to follow it? We return to that useful brainchild of Robert Dilts. If we take Wiseman's findings and fit them into NLLs we find the following:

IDENTITY

The emergent property that derives from the content of the other levels – 'I am lucky.' Suggestions made to this effect are unlikely to be taken on unless the evidence from the levels below identity support them. What needs to be in these other levels for it to be experienced as true to the client?

You might not know at first when you started seeing yourself as a lucky person...it might be some time in the future before you realise that at some point you can't really recall you knew you're a lucky person...in so many ways...when you take the time to do so you find it easier and easier to count the many ways luck is in your life...and the more you count it...the more you can count on it...because everything will turn out well in the end, it just means that obstacles and difficulties are things to look at in a certain way for us to realise the potential they contain...how you can ultimately prosper from anything that comes along...because you're lucky....

BELIEF/VALUES

Lucky belief: A 'My interactions with others will be productive and positive.'

When you and I meet my attitude will affect my behaviour towards you. In turn my behaviour will affect your attitude and that will affect your behaviour towards me. That will then have an effect on my attitude, and so on. It's called the behaviour cycle. If your clients anticipate a positive response from people they interact with they will (more often) create it.

And we don't know when first you realise how people are responding to you differently...in the way that means they're open to your ideas and welcoming of your company...and everybody's different so we don't know yet how often this will happen before you look back and realise you've started to anticipate that people are positive towards you and how much more often something

Fig 10.1

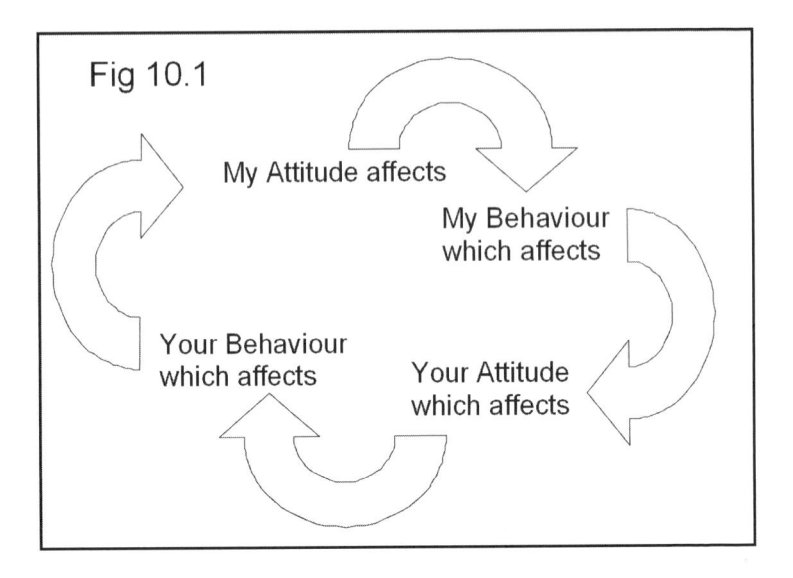

My Attitude affects → My Behaviour which affects → Your Attitude which affects → Your Behaviour which affects → (back to My Attitude)

productive comes from your interactions with people...it becomes easier and easier to believe that it's just the way it is now....

Lucky belief: B 'Good luck is the normal experience for me, so I expect to continue to have it in the future. I will achieve what I set my mind to.'

And you know how one thing leads to another...so it can be with luck...and with so many things changing for you it could be anything that happens you consider being lucky that begins to create more...like a snowball beginning to roll down a hill...more and more luck sticking to it...getting bigger and faster...rolling on until you realise just how much luck you're getting...and because you do how much easier it is to imagine that luck rolling stronger and stronger into the future...as normal a part of your life as anything else....

Familiar territory for you. The trance phenomena of age progression (seeing the future) is a calculation based around the beliefs we've developed over time.

> Lucky belief: C 'Anything that goes wrong will ultimately turn out to be for the good.'
>
> A good thing about getting older is that we learn...if we listen...to experiences because sometimes it takes time to see how things turn out...and yet so often things do...turn out for the best in the long run...or even sooner...so if your unconscious were to be tuning your mind to new opportunities how it means you could begin to believe that everything turns out okay....

In his wide-ranging book *Iron John* Robert Bly explores the subject of manhood. Through metaphor, mythology and folklore he describes the passage from boy to man that has characterised most societies until recent times. Many societies have pain as part of the initiation rite that takes a boy symbolically from boy to man; circumcision among the Jews, some plains tribes who tugged themselves free from hooks that pierced their chests, African tribes who broke a tooth. Bly makes the point that 'from our wound comes our gift...'[13] That made a deep impression. The idea that 'out of your wound comes your genius, out of the thing that hurt you most comes the thing that makes you special' began to inform my work with clients. Many turn up with a sad history, but what if they came to believe that the point of their suffering ultimately led them to the thing that transformed their life wonderfully? I found, often in quite amazing circumstances, that suggesting to them that they look for the gift in their issue led them to liberating insights. The form of the question would usually be something like:

> If everything you'd been through had been for a purpose that would mean (A = B) the rest of your life can be as you'd most want it, what would that purpose be?
>
> If there was something you'd learnt from having your problem that, by learning it (C > E) would mean you could live the rest of your life as you'd like to, what would it be?

It seems that lucky people naturally have this knack of looking for the gift in any situation. I think at some deep level lucky people have a basic assumption that at the end of their life everything will have worked out well. The Rocking-Chair exercise fulfils this for those who don't do it naturally to begin with.

> It can be a really useful skill to find yourself getting better at looking at things in a positive way...that if you were to imagine that everything that happens has positive opportunities...really begin to live as if that's true...everything that happens has a positive side...then it's just a question of how curious you're becoming at looking for the
>
> silver lining...and how your looking means you're getting better and better at finding it...and it doesn't matter if it's you who notices you're looking on the bright side more...or if someone points it out...it's just a good thing that it's happening. And it might not be until the end of the day as you look back on it that you realise just how much more you're feeling positive because you see the possibilities in life...just how much

potential every day contains because it's not the things that happen to us that matter....but what we make of them...and there are so many things we can....

CAPABILITIES

In the previous section I talked about the idea of having a belief that 'out of your wound comes your genius.' What underlies it is the capability to turn something bad into something good. Wiseman identified that lucky people do this naturally. In folk psychology sayings like 'Every cloud has a silver lining' echo the wisdom of being able to see the positive in whatever happens to us. In NLP this is referred to as reframing and is a useful skill to develop as a therapist as well as one to nurture in your clients.

This is helping them become naturally better at seeing opportunity in the twists and turns that life will inevitably throw at them outside of your therapy room. In Appendix 5 I've explored the concept of reframing more deeply. Let's now look at another capability identified by Wiseman worth nurturing.

> 'Lucky people make successful decisions by using their intuition and gut feelings.'

> It is by logic we prove, it is by intuition we discover.
>
> Poincaré

> Also, it became apparent that there were multiple levels of perception and response, not all of which were necessarily at the usual or conscious level of awareness, but were at levels of understanding not recognised by the self, often popularly described as 'instinctive' or 'intuitive'.
>
> Milton Erickson[14]

On the radio I heard a phone-in quiz being conducted by the DJ Neil Fox. The prize was a luxury holiday to Jamaica, and all the participant had to do was listen to a one-second burst of music and identify the group playing it. Neil played the burst. This is the gist of the conversation that took place:

Listener: I'm sorry I don't know who it is.
NF: Oh well, take a guess.
Listener: Honestly, I haven't got a clue.
NF: I know, but it's a holiday to Jamaica, take a leap.
Listener: Really, there's no point, my mind's a blank.
NF: Look, it's a luxury holiday, what's the first group that comes to your mind?
Listener: I don't know...Beautiful South?

It was.

A lucky guess, or some other level of knowing? When I worked at the police training school at Hendon I noticed that most students who went back and changed an answer in their exams usually changed it from right to wrong. It became a mantra, 'Your first answer is your best answer.' What usually happened was that the right answer came to them, but when they went back to it later their self-doubt confused them. They needed to get out of their own way.

The brilliant Scottish physicist James Clerk Maxwell revolutionised science when, with four short equations, he summarised the laws governing electricity and magnetism. Such was the brilliance of these equations that they predicted phenomena that were not discovered until long after his death and caused the Austrian physicist Ludwig Boltzman to exclaim, 'Was it a god that wrote these signs?'

How is such genius possible? Maxwell gave his own answer as he lay dying of cancer: 'What is done by what is called 'myself' is, I feel, done by something greater than myself in me.' He is not alone among great scientists who feel that their discoveries come from layers of the mind over which they have no control.

The chemist Friedrich Kekule von Stradonitz had been working in vain to discover the chemical formula for benzene. Finally the solution came to him as he was staring, exhausted, into his fire. He saw emerging from the flames snakes that turned and bit their own tails. With a sudden flash of insight he saw how the carbon atoms of the benzene molecule linked up to form a ring.

In his excellent book *Hare Brain Tortoise Mind*, Guy Claxton identifies two distinct forms of thinking. The first he calls D-mode (the D standing for deliberation). This is the form of thinking associated with conscious deliberation, weighing up options, interpreting data. We often think of people who are good at this kind of thinking as clever or intelligent. The second mode of thinking is more contemplative, without conscious focus on the solving of the problem. In everyday life when we can't decide what to do we talk about 'sleeping on it'. How often have you done that and woken up the next morning with a decision made? The question is, who made the decision? In Claxton's view, 'Some mysteries can only be penetrated with a relaxed, unquesting mental attitude.'[15]

In Western society the former mode rules. Time is viewed as such an important commodity that ideas and solutions need to be generated quickly, so 'daydreaming' as a form of problem-solving is frowned upon in most businesses – despite the fact that just about any scientific discovery of any note has been achieved by sudden insight – the 'Eureka!' moment, rather than by grinding deliberation. Claxton's view is that this emphasis on conscious knowing has deprived us of an important tool, and I agree with him completely. D-mode, if we are to believe Julian Jaynes, in his book *The Origin of Consciousness in the Breakdown of the Bicameral Mind*, has possibly only been with us for about 4,000 years, yet now we credit it fully with what we achieve. And along the way we have lost contact with a good friend – our unconscious.

Socrates was once observed standing stock still, deep in thought for a full day. When asked what occupied him he replied that he was talking with his daemon. Socrates had an 'inner voice' that advised and led him. Alexander the Great spoke of something similar. It is not so far from Clerk Maxwell's description of his experience, and all lead to Erickson's concept of the unconscious being the source of intuitive wisdom. It's just that by the time we're adults most of us have tuned it out. And yet...have you ever said after something happened, 'I knew that was going to happen,' or, 'Something told me to...'? Inside, the unconscious is striving to be heard, whether by an inner voice, a gut feeling, the flashing of an image. We just have to attune ourselves to it, and teach our clients to do the same. Remember that originally the word *genius* meant a guiding or tutelary spirit. It is useful to think of us *having* a genius rather than *being* a genius, because then you have the freedom to explore it and enjoy it without any of the ego hang-ups that usually come with the territory. In our society how often do the media call someone a genius and then later destroy them because they seem to make the kind of mistakes that ordinary people make? Take David Beckham. He has a genius for football, but out of that context he appears to be an average man of average IQ. Why wouldn't he fall prey to the temptations of an ordinary person placed in his position? If we allowed our heroes to *have* a genius, but *be* human, we wouldn't be disappointed in them anywhere near as often. Add your own examples.

For a long time now I've felt that it wasn't me 'doing' the therapy with my client. Over time it's become my practice to blank my mind and sit and wonder what I'm going to do. I then feel as if I'm observing myself (or the part of myself that's in action) and I'm often amazed at what comes out my mouth. And the moment it does I recognise it as the right thing, but I had no idea it was on its way. So I look to encourage my students and clients to 'get out of their own way', let their unconscious come through as a guide. Watch the world around you, knowing that what parts of the world are in your awareness have been chosen by your unconscious. Become more curious about the choices that are being made: 'Why am I noticing that? Is there something there my unconscious wants me to be aware of?' By practising this I have been surprised at how many instances of 'luck' have come my way. In the greater scheme of things I think a return to valuing more highly our right-brain modes of thinking can only bring us benefit, so we should layer in suggestions to the client about the importance of building a link between the unconscious and conscious, to encourage him/her to trust deeper ways of knowing and doing. Suggestions to achieve this capability could be:

> From today you might find that you're becoming more aware of what's within you...taking time to listen to what your unconscious mind is communicating to you...the more you become aware of this inner wisdom...and its gentle guidance the more you'll realise how you always have this friend within...access to all your learning...guiding you by the things you notice and the things you don't...the things you're doing and the things you don't...getting better every day at spotting the many gentle ways the unconscious speaks to us....
>
> It's such a good thing to know we have access to something within us...something we carry with us...wherever we go we have this intuition...that's always been there...but you might wonder just how you'll start paying closer attention to what it points out...what it is it does that lets you know...what to do...becoming clearer the more

you listen...because most of us have had times when we've known afterwards that something was telling us the right thing to do...and the more you listen to this...the more you find life getting easier and better....

BEHAVIOUR

I once had a client who was heavily into self-development. She'd been on all kinds of courses and through many forms of therapy before she knocked on my door. We worked through the issues she presented, which revolved around self-esteem and confidence, and I quickly got the feeling that we were going in circles. The same stuff kept coming up and there was no perceived improvement. This lady had actually given up work so she could spend more time 'developing herself', so I asked her, what did she do with her day? She looked at me quizzically and said, 'Well, I work on myself.'

'Yes, but what do you actually do with your day?'

This went in the same circle a couple of times before she got the point of my question.

'Well, I spend most of my time in my room (she lived with her parents), you know, working on myself.'

'So, how would you know that you'd changed, what could actually be different in your life that you'd notice?'

'I'd feel different about myself.'

'In regard to what?'

That stumped her. Her contacts with people were minimal, her opportunities to calibrate any improvement in her confidence were just about non-existent. It's like an Olympic sprinter training all winter in the gym. She's not going to know if she can run any faster until she leaves the gym and gets on the track. All therapy has to involve the client 'doing' in-between sessions. Wiseman suggests that the most effective things for them to be doing to improve their perception of the world –

i.e., to feel luckier within it – are the following:

1 Build networks. Most opportunities in life arise from our contacts with others. It is estimated that on average we all know about 300 people. Through those people we have access to 90,000 (300 times 300) others. If each of the people in our network introduced us to just one person in theirs then this doubles to 180,000. The principle here is simple, encourage your clients to create opportunities for meeting people. Of course, the principle is simple but if your client is heavily introverted or has some manifestation of social phobia then new behaviours like suddenly going to a busy bar may be too much. Again, we avoid dictating how they build their network, we only prime them to find their own way.

There are many ways to increase opportunities in your life…opportunities that surround us all…and no way is right for everyone…so if your unconscious mind were just to begin to make you aware of possibilities…that you could safely explore…it might surprise you what comes to your mind…what ideas seem possible…to meet people…to learn new things …create changes….

And if there was just one thing that you began to do that increased your circle…that enabled you to safely expand your possibilities…it doesn't actually matter what that thing turns out to be…and whether it's what you would have expected it to be or if it's something completely new…it's only important that it happens….

2 Vary routines. We're all creatures of habit, we're made that way. Most of us are comfortable in our routines because they provide us with what they're intended to. Our clients are likely to have created routines that maintain their problem. Indeed a while ago I identified something I called the therapeutic paradox, a strange fact that behaviours we generate often create the opposite of what they were intended for. You can read about it in Appendix 1. One of my graduates, Penny Pyke, came up with a great idea with her clients that really seems to work. Penny gets the clients to identify all the habits they have related to the problem; where they tend to do their problem, how they tend to do it, etc. For example, with smokers she might identify that they smoke most when they're around people, that their favourite fags are the first in the morning with a cup of coffee and with a pint in their hand in the evening, and that they normally hold the cigarette in their right hand. Penny will get the clients to come up with a way to change every habit – not necessarily stop the habit, just disrupt it. So the clients will smoke less when with people and smoke more when they're on their own; they'll start the day with a cup of peppermint tea instead of coffee; smoke with their left hand, drink bitter instead of lager. This can be a tremendous way of retuning the clients' awareness of what's around them. Get clients to change their route to work, the time they go to the gym, eat dinner, the programmes they watch on TV – but prime them with a purpose.

Erickson was famous for the tasks he gave people, the most famous of which was getting them to hike to the top of Squaw Peak, a local beauty spot. Often clients would report dramatic insights about their problem. How did this happen? The human brain looks for patterns, remember? When clients come to a therapist they do so in a state of expectation – especially if the therapist is someone as famous as Erickson. Everything the therapist says, does, or asks them to do is primed with the unconscious question, 'What has this to do with why I've come here?' So a strenuous walk to the top of a mountain is suddenly imbued with deeper meaning – 'What might I find?' And because the thinker thinks there's something to find the prover will generally find it. So when you suggest variations to routine it needs to be linked in your suggestion to what changes to their problem these variations might (not will) create. Whatever differences they bring back to the next session you incorporate into the change-link pattern.

> You can probably appreciate that if we keep doing what we've always done we'll keep ending up with what we've always had…and from today you could try not to notice the habits that are part of your problem and notice that you can't…so as you see them more and more it might amaze you just how many new ways you can find for doing new things….
>
> So as you begin to do things in new ways…just having fun mixing and changing…your unconscious mind is becoming aware of what this means about how you're changing…and it might not be until afterwards that you realise what a difference these differences are making to you….

3 The American millionaire and onetime would-be presidential candidate Ross Perot once said, 'Most people give up just as they're about to achieve success. They give up in the last minute of the game one foot from a winning touchdown.' Wiseman identified that lucky people persevere. They keep going when others give up – probably because they have a belief that things will turn out okay so the pleasure principle continues to motivate them towards the pleasure of achievement, rather than away from the expectation of failure. Lucky people also don't dwell on failures, they move on. Ask a pessimist about his past and he'll tell you about all the bad things that have happened to him, ask an optimist and the opposite is true. The NLP presupposition 'There is no failure, only feedback' is so useful it should be available as an implant.

> Someone once said to me that things aren't supposed to be easy…just possible…and if you were to cast your mind back…as far back as it

needs to go...to remember something you've done that you found difficult at first...but which by persevering paid off in the longer run...there might be more than one such time...all adding up to realising how you can...keep going...and just remaining open to what you can learn from a difficulty that means you can get through it...growing as you learn...to persevere...sticking with where you're going because you're listening to your unconscious mind.

And the more you see what your goal is the more you find you can move through any difficulties that appear...focussing on what lies beyond them...is your goal...achieved....

ENVIRONMENT

The elements from behaviour give us the idea of what environment people who are primed to be lucky operate within. Opportunities for social connection are vital, for your clients to begin to feel more fortunate in the life they're living they must enhance the network they operate within, or make more use of the one they're in. They must also embrace novelty, take themselves to new places, or look for new experiences within their current environment.

It might not be straightaway that you begin to notice around you things that take your interest, and you might wonder if they were always there and why it's now that they're there...what might they bring you...that's new and interesting or exciting.

And there are many people around...every day...and if you were to become more and more curious about them...the opportunities that surround us...what a novelty it might start out as until it just becomes...so natural to be a part of what brings to you the things that feel good...that feel right...now you can safely put only as much effort into enhancing your connection to the world as begins to bring you those new enriching opportunities.

So we can both wonder what will be the first thing your mind makes you aware of that is new to you...an idea...or thought...a chance...meeting of minds...or eyes...that just makes you wonder where it might lead towards your goal...and this curiosity can grow stronger the more you notice these new things happening around you...always there...for you to choose from...trusting whatever it is that guides you towards one thing over another....

Now we can take the suggestions I created for each NLL, and join them together using the Wordweaving™ rule that seventy per cent of a suggestion pattern should be aimed at environment, behaviour or capability and that these are then linked with suggestions aimed at belief/values and identity, usually by using a complex equivalence or cause-and-effect conjunction.

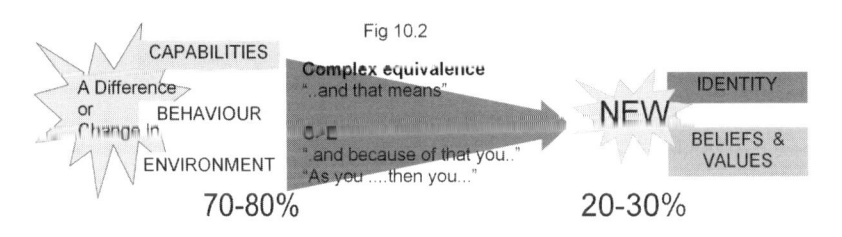

Fig 10.2

CAPABILITIES
A Difference or Change in
BEHAVIOUR
ENVIRONMENT
70-80%

Complex equivalence
"...and that means"
C-E
"...and because of that you..."
"As you ....then you..."

NEW
IDENTITY
BELIEFS & VALUES
20-30%

One variation of many would be the following (I've provided a key so you can follow the use of the levels. **E** = Environment, **B** = Behaviour, **C** = Capabilities, **Beliefs** = Beliefs, **V** = Values, **I** = Identity):

> **C** And there is no way of knowing, yet, how, just by listening, you become more aware that there are many ways to increase opportunities in your life...opportunities that surround us all...and no way is right for everyone...so if your unconscious mind were just to begin to make you aware of possibilities...that you could safely explore...it might surprise you what comes to your mind...what ideas seem possible...to meet people...to learn new things...create changes....
>
> **B** And if there was just one thing that you began to do that increased your circle...that enabled you to safely expand your possibilities...it doesn't actually matter what that thing turns out to be...and whether it's what you would have expected it to be or if it's something completely new...it's only important that it happens....
>
> **E** So we can both wonder what will be the first thing your mind makes you aware of that is new to you...an idea...or thought...a chance...meeting of minds...or eyes...that just makes you wonder where it might lead towards your goal...and this curiosity can grow stronger the more you notice these new things happening around you...are always there...for you to choose from...trusting whatever it is that guides you towards one thing over another...because...

I you might not know at first when you started seeing yourself as a lucky person...it might be some time in the future before you realise that at some point you can't really recall you knew you're a lucky person...in so many ways...when you take the time to do so you find it easier and easier to count the many ways luck is in your life...and the more you count it...the more you can count on it...because everything will turn out well in the end it just means that obstacles and difficulties are things to look at in a certain way for us to realise the potential they contain...how you can ultimately prosper from anything that comes along...because you're lucky.

C So you might find that you're becoming more aware of what's within you...taking time to listen to what your unconscious mind is communicating to you...the more you become aware of this inner wisdom...and its gentle guidance...the more you'll realise how you always have this friend within...access to all your learning...guiding you by the things you notice and the things you don't...the things you're doing and the things you don't...getting better every day at spotting the many gentle ways the unconscious speaks to us...

B...because you can probably appreciate that if we keep doing what we've always done we'll keep ending up with what we've always had...and from today you could try not to notice the habits that are part of your problem and notice that you can't...so as you see them more and more it might amaze you just how many new ways you can find for doing new things...

E...and it might not be straightaway you notice around you things that take in your interest, and you might wonder if they were always there and why it's now that they're there...what might they bring you...that's new and interesting or exciting...

Belief...that just means that it might not be until the end of the day as you look back on it that you realise just how much more you're feeling positive because you see the possibilities in life...just how much potential every day contains because it's not the things that happen to us that matter...but what we make of them...and there are so many things we can...

C...there are so many ways to increase opportunities in your life...opportunities that surround us all...and no way is right for everyone...so if your unconscious mind were just to begin to make you aware of possibilities...that you could safely explore...it might surprise you what comes to your mind...what ideas seem possible...to meet people...to learn new things...create changes....

BC And the more you see what your goal is the more you find you can move through any difficulties that appear...focussing on what lies beyond them...is your goal achieved...

C...and it's a good thing to remember something someone once said to me...that things aren't supposed to be easy...just possible...and if you were to cast your mind back...as far back as it needs to go...to remember something you've done that you found difficult at first...but which by persevering paid off in the longer run...there might be more than one such time...all adding up to realising how you can...keep going...and just remaining open to what you can learn from a difficulty that means you can get through it...growing as you learn...to persevere....sticking with where you're going because you are listening to your unconscious mind...

C...and it's such a good thing to know we have access to something within us...something we carry with us...wherever we go we have this intuition...that's always been there...but you might be curious just how you'll start paying closer attention to what it points out...what it is it does that lets you know...what to do...becoming clearer the more you listen...because most of us have had times when we've known afterwards that something was telling us the right thing to do...and the more you listen to this...the more you find life getting easier and better....

E So who knows what will be the first thing your mind makes you aware of that is new to you...an idea...or thought...a chance...meeting of minds...or eyes...that just makes you wonder where it might lead towards your goal...and this curiosity can grow stronger the more you notice these new things happening around you...always there...for you to choose from...trusting whatever it is that guides you towards one thing over another...

C...because it can be a really useful skill to find yourself getting better at looking at things in a positive way...that if you were to imagine that everything that happens has positive opportunities...really begin to live as if that's true...everything that happens has a positive side...then it's just a question of how curious you're becoming at looking for the silver lining...and how your looking means you're getting better and better at finding it...and it doesn't matter if it's you who notices you're looking on the bright side more...or if someone points it out...it's just a good thing that it's happening...

Belief...because when you realise how people are responding to you differently...in the way that means they're open to your ideas and welcoming of your company...and everybody's different so we don't know yet how often this will happen before you look back and realise you've started to anticipate that people are positive towards you and how much more often something productive comes from your interactions with people...it becomes easier and easier to believe that it's just the way it is now.

E And there are so many people around...every day...that if you were to become more and more curious about them...the opportunities that surround you...what a novelty it might start out as until it just becomes...so natural to be a part of what brings to you the things that feel good...that feel right...now you can safely put only as much effort into enhancing your connection to the world as begins to bring you those new enriching opportunities.

B So as you begin to do things in new ways...just having fun mixing and changing...your unconscious mind is becoming aware of what this means about how you're changing...and it might not be until afterwards that you realise what a difference these differences are making to you.

Belief And you know how one thing leads to another...so it can be with luck...and with so many things changing for you it could be anything that happens you consider being lucky that begins to create more...like a snowball beginning to roll down a hill...more and more luck sticking to it...getting bigger and faster...rolling on until you realise just how much luck you're getting...and because you do how much easier it is to imagine that luck rolling stronger and stronger into the future...as normal a part of your life as anything else...normal to be lucky....

If I were mathematically inclined I'd be able to tell you how many different suggestion patterns can be created by combining the suggestions from each level in different orders, but I'm not, so the best I can say is that it would be a lot. Certainly enough to fill the twenty to twenty-five minutes that I've suggested is the optimal time for a suggestion session. The great flexibility of suggestions built in to the Wordweaving™ style is its ease in linking them together, because they avoid content – they just create opportunities for clients to prime their mind to their own evidence for change, rather than the evidence that your idea of an opportunity provides.

Priming your clients to anticipate a world of opportunity can provide a major shift in their model of the world. I don't know if the mind creates the universe it lives in as some suggest, but I do believe the mind creates the universe it thinks it lives in. So why not create a world where luck and opportunity abound, and you feel empowered to seize those opportunities and live an amazing life? If clients were to feel luckier in life how much more likely would they be to believe in the improvements you're helping them to create? I'm aware that I'm stepping into a turf war between two different philosophies, realism and pragmatism. In simple terms realism says that if you're walking round with a bad haircut people should tell you – it's better to live in reality, even if it makes you unhappy. Pragmatism suggests that it's better not to be told about your haircut and live in happy ignorance of reality. My view is that seeing that we're not equipped to know anything more than a pale version of reality we have a great deal of freedom in creating it in the most positive way. There are as many realities as there are living things. None of them is true – so let's live in the happiest illusion and help our clients do the same.

Conclusion

By taking Helen through the four stages of therapy this book has described, as the context of her problem has been reframed, its structure adapted and its pattern interrupted by the techniques I've used and the wordweaving suggestions I've made, I've been able to use the change-link pattern to consolidate her improvements and the luck pattern and Rocking-Chair exercise to prime her mind to anticipate a positive consequence of the work we've done together. The day arrives when:

T: So, when you think about what you came here for...are we there?

H: Well, I certainly think I'm well on my way.

T: On a scale of nought to ten, where's your confidence in those situations where you used to have a problem?

H: Oh, I would say about an eight – sometimes probably a nine.

T: Good. And it seems to be continuing to get better.

H: Yes, it does. Like everyone I have my bad days, but overall I feel very different.

T: So do you think there's anything else for us to accomplish for now or do you want to see how things go?

H: I think it'd be good to leave it for a while and see how I get on. I can always call if things start to slip.

T: Sure, and they probably won't. Life will happen and we all stumble from time to time but what I find with clients who've made the kinds of changes you have is that when you have a bad day, it somehow doesn't mean what it used to. Somehow something's changed in you and you respond differently and get better at doing that as time goes on. And if anything else comes up just give me a call [suggestions to the end!].

Then...exit to violins playing the theme to *Little House on the Prairie*.

So we've taken Helen through a successful example of therapy, from a place where the world supported her limitations, to a world where she's tuned to noticing those things that enhance her sense of wellness. Along the way I've simplified the interactions, not mentioned the postponed appointments and the days when Helen wasn't ready for anything more than gentle conversational reframing – some days it's legitimate to chat when you pick up the signs that the client's unconscious doesn't want to play today. But the beauty of Wordweaving™ is that within any conversation you have the tools to tap gently at the pattern as it appears in what the clients say. Chat, but chat with a purpose, always. Perhaps a summary of the philosophy of Wordweaving™ is contained within this meta-modelled dialogue:

> Wordweaving™ is a process.
> *For what?*
> To help clients change their perceptions about their problem.
> *To what?*
> To whatever it needs to be for them not to have their problem.
> *How does it do that?*
> By providing the means by which clients create whatever meanings to their experiences, past, present and future, that free them from their limitations. The therapist provides no content, only a framework for the client to explore and create or adapt beliefs.

One thing left to provide for you is the set of techniques and interventions we employ within Cognitive Hypnotherapy to help the clients adjust their pattern. For me Wordweaving™ provides the glue that connects the changes the techniques create and links them to the 'future clients' who **are** their solution state. It assists in adjusting the perceptions of the 'present client' that support the neurological changes that I believe good techniques create. Suggestions on their own have a lower chance of long-term success, and techniques on their own the same. Used together one supports the other.

In Volume III, *Wordweaving™ The Past Participant* I'll provide the theory that supports the use of regression and the most effective techniques I've found to change negative memories. It will also contain interventions to reframe the context of a problem pattern, interventions to change its structure and interventions to interrupt the process. I'll also be talking more about working in all three time frames to fully support our clients in their pursuit of personal happiness.

I hope this book has taken you further along your path. As it's appeared before me on my PC I've recognised the concept I've termed Cognitive Hypnotherapy becoming clearer and helping me move along mine. It's probably appropriate to finish by attempting a summation from what has developed within these first two volumes of what I consider Cognitive Hypnotherapy to be.

Whenever I'm asked what Cognitive Hypnotherapy is I normally have to start with what it isn't. It isn't an approach that sees trance as a special state, certainly not one created by the hypnotist. It does not believe that depth of trance is a significant factor in the success of a suggestion or technique, or that trance is necessarily a state of relaxation – some trance states are packed to the gills with fear, anxiety, panic and any others that can jam themselves in. It does not believe that the therapist's role is to come up with answers, only questions that guide the client to finding his or her own.

Let's start with Orr's Law, because it has such an important place. In many important respects the world is what we believe it to be. If our Thinker thinks something is true, then our Prover will bring information to the foreground that confirms it, and leave in the background everything that contradicts it. This filtering of information is achieved by what Bandler and Grinder described as 'universal modeling processes', deletion, distortion and generalisation. I've suggested that these three processes correspond to the nine major trance phenomena – they are how the mind deletes, distorts and generalises. This places trance centrally in the normal spectrum of human experience. We spend much, if not most of our time in states woven from these phenomena and it is from these states that many of the patterns that form our belief systems arise. Trance phenomena are a fundamental part of the problem pattern of the client, and a fundamental part of the solution. In many respects Cognitive Hypnotherapy involves waking the client up from the trance he/she is in while 'doing' his/her problem, or at least helping create a more pleasant trance.

Much of our brain is devoted to identifying patterns of information from our surroundings. It uses our interpretation of our past experiences to give meaning to our present and to calculate the possible consequences to us in the future. I suggest that the mind uses three basic algorithms to perform these calculations: $A=B$, $C>E$ and $A=\text{not }B$. In simple terms the purpose of these calculations is Freud's *Pleasure Principle* – our unconscious seeks to move us towards pleasure and away from pain.

However, problems arise because our mind is modular, not singular. We have an executive module that we feel is our 'self', our authentic identity. This module lives under the illusion that it controls all of our actions and plots our course through life. It doesn't, most of what we do is the result of unconscious processes and drives, our 'I' just spins a convincing story to itself (and anyone else who'll listen) about why it's spent its life the way it has.

The unconscious is part of this modularity, there is no single unconscious in conflict with the conscious, rather a host of 'parts' that perform a particular function or are triggered into action by particular circumstances. Problems are often caused by the inner conflict between these conscious and unconscious parts, or where a part is using a particular interpretation of past information that creates a limiting version of present reality. How they come to do so is explained by the tenets of Cognitive Psychology. It has two main organising themes:

- Actions are caused by mental processes.
- The mind is a computer.

Let's look at both of these in turn, and if you are a technophobe, don't panic because we are not going to mention gigabytes, googlebots or teraflops once.

Actions are caused by mental processes

Psychology is the science of human behaviour. Its project is to understand why humans act in the way they do. Cognitive psychology proposes that we are all psychologists, seeking to understand our actions, and the actions of others. From the earliest days we are trying to work out what's going on and why.

As such we are creatures who seek meaning, and, just as we believe that everything that happens around us has a cause – I get wet because I walk in the rain, my dog barks because it has heard something outside – so we attribute our behaviour to our mental processes (thoughts) – 'I got angry because I thought my girlfriend looked at someone else,' 'I laughed because I thought someone falling over in front of me was funny.' For most people this is not news. It broadly corresponds to how 'folk' psychology has operated, probably for hundreds of years. What is different is the precision with which cognitive psychology describes these mental processes. It calls them computations, I tend to use the term *calculations* and use the idea of the *three algorithms* as the means by which the mind (or part of it) makes the calculation.

The mind is a computer
This does not mean that the mind uses the operating principles of a computer, like the use of binary code. We know it doesn't. Basing themselves on the work of British mathematician Alan Turing, Cognitive Psychologists define a computer as a set of operations for processing information.

This is an important distinction to make, because it means that the computer is software, not hardware. The essence of a computer does not lie in the materials from which it is made, but in the programs it executes. You need a machine to run it on, but you could use many different types of machine. The mind is thus a very complicated program, which they seek to describe in terms of information processing, without needing to focus on how the brain (the hardware) actually does it. In the words of Dylan Evans and Oscar Zarate, 'The key to behaviour is the program, not the materials out of which the machine is made.'[16]

From this idea we could envisage the mind as a series of programs that develop from both a genetic base and as a reaction to experience. Wolinsky would probably describe these programs as trance identities, the followers of Fritz Perls would probably call them parts. My sons would probably say, 'Whatever!' And that's right. The term we use isn't as important as the idea it conveys; that our mind is made of different programs that have different agendas. There is more than one ghost in the machine. Sometimes these differences cause conflict. Trance phenomena are the means by which each program/trance identity creates the illusion of reality it requires to perform its function.

We look to evolutionary psychology for the basis of this conflict between different programs. The premise of Evolutionary Psychology is that, if Cognitive Psychology shows us that the mind exhibits a very complex design (there are more connections between cells in the brain than stars in the universe), whose purpose is to process different forms of information, and evolutionary biology tells us that complex designs in nature come about only by natural selection, then the design of the mind must have evolved by a process of natural selection – i.e., each part of the mind has been created by mutation, and retained because of its usefulness in solving particular problems.

None of these mutations is likely to have arisen in the last 10,000 years. The brain and mind we have is adapted to solve the physical and social problems that arise from life in a small group of hunter-gatherers on the savannah. The most important adaptive problems in this environment are thought to be:

- Avoiding predators.
- Eating the right food.
- Forming alliances and friendships.
- Providing help to children and other relatives.
- Reading other people's minds.
- Communicating with other people.
- Selecting mates.

All of the abilities shown above are crucial for passing on your genes. That being the case, evolution should have designed mental *modules* to achieve these objectives in the ancestral environment.

These modules obviously continue to have a use within the modern situation, but, bearing in mind that their purpose is processing information, if the wrong computation is made then the behaviour the module generates as a result is likely to be wrong as well. Beside each module I have put a 'software fault' that **might** be attributed to it.

- Avoiding predators – phobias.
- Eating the right food – eating disorders, weight problems.
- Forming alliances and friendships – low self-esteem, jealousy, insecurity.
- Providing help to children and other relatives – guilt.
- Reading other people's minds – paranoia.
- Communicating with other people – alienation, social phobias.
- Selecting mates – jealousy, insecurity.

I introduce them to you now only to get you thinking about the modular nature of the brain, and how these faults can be likened to software errors (like computer viruses). The purpose of Cognitive Hypnotherapy becomes one of debugging the programs that aren't working for the client, and so enabling a greater sense of congruency in their daily lives. Each program has a pattern that contains information about context, structure, process and consequence. This is what makes up the thought the Thinker has that the Prover seeks to prove. Changing part of the pattern changes the operation of the program and may render its purpose completely redundant.

Our brain is an expensive investment by evolution – it consumes thirty per cent of our daily calories. It doesn't make sense that the reward of this investment would be behaviours less likely to help us survive – unhappiness isn't hardwired. Our problems are simply mistakes based on the brain's miscalculations – usually when our computer is too young to make good ones. The young brain is only capable of a limited complexity in its calculations, labelled by the educationalist Piaget as 'nominal processing' – things are black or white, good or bad, right or wrong. As we mature we become capable of finer levels of rationality and understanding, but unfortunately the results of our earlier struggles to comprehend the world and keep us safe continue to provide the basis for later calculations – just as the programming errors of early versions of Microsoft Windows continue to cause crashes in later versions – so problems that start as SEEs to a juvenile generalise into debilitating adult problems. An important principle here is that the programs running these problems **have a positive intention** – they're a program trying to help, just in the wrong way – remember Mrs Toothbrush from Volume I? This applies with a wide range of issues, from phobias to smoking (why would we be motivated to do something that's going to kill us unless at some level part of us thought there was a benefit?). Cognitive Hypnotherapy is constantly looking for better ways to assist the client in recoding the programs that don't work for him or her. Wordweaving™ is a central part of it because it offers a model that utilises the trance phenomena that form the problem as a means of changing it.

Essentially what Cognitive Hypnotherapy seeks to do is identify what the thinker thinks that causes the problem. This is the problem pattern. We change it in any way possible and then prime the mind to link this change to a continuing movement towards the solution state – **the client's world without the client's issue.**

Finally, I would add to the philosophy some of the presuppositions of NLP that have guided me for a long time:

1 The map is not the territory

The words we use are NOT the event or the item they represent. Our perception of reality is not reality itself – only our individual version of it. We all have developed our own map or model of the world in response to the experiences we have had and how we have felt about them. We use this model to navigate life. Difficulties occur when our map is too rigid; when it is missing information; when it is different from the map of the person we are talking to, or when it is distorted. We can think of our map as being the sum total of the calculations our mind has made. Each of our trance identities/parts/programs potentially works from a different map. Personal development involves creating the best single map of the best reality we want to live in – but know that it's still just a map of it.

2 Respect for the other person's model of the world

All clients have reasons valid to them for seeing the world in the way they do. It is not for the therapist to make the clients accept the therapist's model, but to enable the clients to enrich their own model in any way which improves their life.

3 Resistance in a client is a sign of a lack of rapport

There are no resistant clients, only inflexible communicators. Effective communicators accept and utilise all communication presented to them.

4 People are not their behaviours

Accept the person, change the behaviour. Most people confuse this point. How many parents say 'Bad boy/girl!' when they actually mean 'Bad behaviour!'?

5 All are doing the best they can with the resources they have available

Behaviour is geared for adaptation, and present behaviour is the best choice available. Every behaviour is motivated by a positive intent. This is a really big concept to grasp. Can a serial killer really have a positive intention? For him he can. This idea is about unconscious motivation. I work on the basis that the unconscious is a protective device that seeks to learn what it can from any negative situation in order to prevent it happening again. I have consistently found that behaviour clients wish to change is generated by the unconscious with the intention of helping. I'll give an example.

In an extreme case like a serial killer the decisions made by the young unconscious, in response to what is often quite profound trauma, tends to be reinforced by subsequent experiences. As a result his actions become more and more maladapted – while still trying to fulfil a positive intention like being in control, having company, not feeling inferior, etc.

6 You can be more in charge of your mind, and therefore your results

Many in NLP would say: 'You are in charge.' I hope to show that being in charge is an illusion created by our conscious, and that most of our behaviour is generated by unconscious processes completely out of our awareness. One of the benefits of NLP is that it enables us to shine light more often on these processes to give us more, but never total, control.

7   People have all the resources they need to succeed and to achieve their desired outcomes

There are no unresourceful people, only unresourceful states. This comes directly from the philosophy of Erickson. As therapists we do not 'give' the client anything, we assist him/her in rediscovering his/her own resources.

I think of us as tour guides helping our clients find within themselves skills, strengths, and abilities they have always had but that negative experiences have blocked them from. Imagine that at birth we have this golden seed inside us that, if fed by a constant stream of positive experiences, would grow into something that completely fulfils its potential. Now find someone with a childhood full of only those experiences! In practice the young shoot gets diverted, distorted and twisted by its environment into a more limited version of its original potential. Given different childhood experiences we would all be different people. The good news is that, as Richard Bandler once said: 'It is never too late to have a happy childhood' (or at least one free of the bad decisions we made about ourselves during it).

8 There is no failure, only feedback

This is one of my favourites and one that I put as a screen saver on my children's computer. They repaid me by telling me how Thomas Edison, while pursuing a workable electric light bulb, conducted 10,000 experiments without success. A friend said to him, 'Thomas, you must feel terrible to have failed 10,000 times.' Edison looked at him quizzically and replied, 'I haven't failed once, I've found 10,000 ways it doesn't work.'

During his lifetime he patented over 1,600 devices. How many would he if he had believed in failure? When something doesn't work out, find out why, and move on. The meaning of not succeeding is only the positive learning you get from it. That's a useful belief to work from when you're working with clients.

That's a brief summation of the main principles of Cognitive Hypnotherapy. I'm sure I'll add to them as my journey continues, a journey I hope I've interested you in accompanying me on.

Trevor Silvester

The important thing in science is not so much to obtain new facts as to discover new ways of thinking about them...

Lawrence Bragg

Appendices

Appendix 1

The therapeutic paradox (originally published in the Hypnotherapy Journal, *Summer 2001)*

Miss X arrives in my office complaining that she never meets nice men. Investigation uncovers her fear of being hurt. How is it that with this fear she keeps ending up in abusive relationships?

Mr Y finds himself increasingly isolated socially because he smokes, yet we establish that his unconscious motivation to smoke began when he was fourteen and wanted to belong to the 'in crowd'. Why does the unconscious cause a behaviour that brings the opposite of its intention?

I have found this paradoxical pattern in many of my clients. Research has suggested that ninety per cent of our daily behaviour is produced unconsciously. If that *is* the case why would the unconscious produce behaviour that ends up with the opposite of what it desires, and keep on doing it?

An explanation requires certain assumptions. The first is that behaviour is purposeful. From the point of view of evolutionary psychology our actions are designed to assist the survival of our genes. From that perspective all behaviour has a positive intention for the individual. Our unconscious moves us towards pleasurable experiences, and away from negative ones – or ones it perceives will be negative based on previous experience (the pleasure principle).

The second presupposition is that we are creatures who seek meaning. Nothing is allowed to 'just happen'. From the earliest age we are looking to make sense of the world, to make it predictable. Cognitive psychology suggests that we act as scientists, forming personal hypotheses about the way the world works, and creating behaviour that is appropriate to these beliefs. Dr Leonard Orr suggests a dual mental mechanism of 'the thinker' and 'the prover'. He suggests that once the thinker has developed a belief about any aspect of existence, the prover will adjust the input from our senses to validate the belief. The maxim is: 'What the thinker thinks, the prover proves.'

The third presupposition is that the unconscious acts as a protective device, using previous events in our life to determine appropriate action in the present. An easy illustration of this is to describe a phobia using these presuppositions:

A man came to see me with a fear of fish. He couldn't even watch the Goldfish credit card advert on TV. Using Cognitive Hypnotherapy I regressed him to the first event connected to the problem. He recalled a time when he was three when his father came home early in the morning from a night of sea fishing. As some fathers do he thought it would be funny to make his son jump, so he put his catch (which sounded like a conger eel) on his son's bed. The little boy felt the weight of it and opened his eyes – to find the face of the eel inches from his. As you can imagine it scared the life out of him.

Now, working with the assumptions I began with, his unconscious needs to protect him from any similarly 'dangerous' occasions. At that age, as the work of Swiss educationalist Piaget demonstrated, a child's logical ability is limited to what is termed 'nominal processing'. This equates to 'this is better than that,' 'this is because of that,' 'this is right, that is wrong,' etc. Using this level of sophistication the unconscious searches for black and white causation: 'What has caused this fear? It must be the fish. If I keep you away from fish you will be safe.' Thus, this

SEE acts as a reference point for the unconscious to measure threat in the future. Every time he comes into contact with a fish, or anticipates doing so, his unconscious kicks the fight or flight response into action to get him away from the danger (or to kill it).

Because this event is stored unconsciously he is not aware of this mental computation, only of the result – an overwhelming emotional response – proximity to a fish causes what he describes as a 'panic attack'. The intention is to protect him; the result is to inappropriately restrict his life. Remember, I said the unconscious is there to protect you, not necessarily to make you happy. Every time he confronts a fish and emerges unscathed because of the response it reinforces it (what the thinker thinks…).

That is a simple illustration of part of the model that produces the paradox, not the paradox itself. The next part of the model is to do with the way perceptions are shaped. Two factors are central:

> **1** Don't think of a blue tree. What came to your mind? Your mind cannot process negatives, so to 'not think of something' it has to think of it. It is the structure of craving. Imagine someone who is trying to diet saying to herself, 'I mustn't have that cake/biscuit/chocolate.' The negative structure of that thought forces her to think of eating. Repeating that structure through a whole day brings you to the point of obsession about that chocolate chip cookie!

> **2** The concept of foreground and background. The picture you can see is probably familiar to you. Some see the young lady, some the old. An interesting question is who decided which one you

saw? The answer is, your unconscious. It processed the picture and gave it meaning, and produced one version for your conscious awareness. It did not say to your conscious, 'I've got a choice here, which one do you want?'

Knowing there are two options most of you will be able to switch between both versions, but you cannot see both simultaneously. That is the gestalt principle of figure and ground; whichever one you focus on is the figure, which sends the other option into the background with all other possible information available to your senses. Those of you with any contact with NLP will be aware that your unconscious filters 2,000,000 bits of information every second. Conscious awareness can only handle approximately seven bits per second, so your unconscious is making figure/ground decisions on a grand scale every second.

The final part of the paradox model is the formation of beliefs. For the purpose of this article I will take a belief to be a generalisation about yourself, or the world, based on experiences or lessons delivered by people significant to us, such as 'I'm no good,' or 'The world is a tough place.' In the words of John Burton

> Almost all, if not all, limiting beliefs about self, others or life form during childhood.[17]

In the main this is the first twelve years of life.

So let's return to Miss X. At five years old her parents divorce. The father she adores moves out. At five years old children place themselves at the centre of the universe, and are the 'cause' of the things going on around them. It is a common experience to find that the five-year-old blames herself – 'If only I'd been better he would have stayed.' She feels generally insecure and her unconscious looks for something to make her feel better. She attaches strongly to her maternal grandfather, who is loving and kind towards her. At nine years old her grandfather dies suddenly of a heart attack. Another loving male figure has left her suddenly.

The task of the unconscious is to keep her away from negative experiences. Finding the similarity between these two SEEs, it forms the belief: 'Men you love leave, don't let them close.' Emotionally this is stored as a fear of getting hurt.

As the years go by her behaviour falls into a pattern. The dominant aspect of herself, the maturing woman with a healthy sexual appetite, finds herself attracted to, and attracting men. However, she finds that as soon as it begins to develop into something meaningful she finds herself withdrawing. Worse still, her unconscious is fixated on avoiding men who will hurt her. Men likely to do this are the 'foreground', men who are not likely to hurt her are the 'background' and so are hardly noticed by her. It appears to Miss X that the world is full of 'bad men', and the best she can do is pick the best of the worst. By the time she comes to see me she has a history of broken relationships, is scared of committing, and has been hurt repeatedly.

Here is the therapeutic paradox: Miss X arrives with a fear of getting hurt. The behaviour her unconscious generates to protect her actually manifests the hurt she is desperate to avoid. These are the dangers of a well-intentioned unconscious mind using archaic beliefs as a reference for present action. I hope the story demonstrates all three of my presuppositions.

With Mr Y the story follows the same paradoxical lines. When a young man he was quite small and was often picked on. Children fear rejection by their peers and will go to great lengths to avoid it. The repetition of being excluded and made to feel stupid because of his size leads to a feeling of insecurity and of 'not belonging'. He becomes one of those boys who fall in with a gang and do whatever the leaders suggest in order to 'belong'. He gets into trouble and becomes disruptive. Teachers describe him as 'easily led'. At twelve behind the bike sheds he is offered the next level of 'belonging' – a cigarette! His initial refusal is met with jeers. The message to his unconscious is clear: 'smoking equals belonging, not smoking equals rejection'. There is no contest. He begins to smoke. Twenty years later he comes to me to give up. He has tried on many occasions, but always ends up giving in. He describes to me how nowadays in his work environment and even at home, he ends up smoking outside alone. It makes him miserable, but somehow he ends up smoking more.

Here again is the paradox in action: Mr Y's motivation for smoking is his fear of 'not belonging'. Now, as an adult, the action of smoking tends to isolate him from the people he wants to belong to (i.e. his friends and partner). This triggers the fear. His unconscious associates the act of smoking with belonging, so, in effect says to him: 'Go on then, have a fag, you'll feel better ' The cycle continues. I have come across the paradox in similar forms connected with issues of comfort; company; belonging; being loved, and many others in relation to both smoking and weight issues. In essence this suggests that just dealing with the symptom – the smoking – is unlikely to succeed. Work on the underlying issue that provides the motivation to smoke, and success is more likely. It will also have a much greater impact on the smoker's life.

Listening out for the paradox in the 'script' of your clients: the very problem they are complaining about may be caused by their unconscious attempts to avoid it.

Appendix 2

NLLs

The relationship between identity and beliefs, and then their relationship to our abilities and behaviour, is usefully described by a model that Robert Dilts created from work initiated by Gregory Bateson, which Dilts calls NLLs. I think it is one of the most useful, and least used, models in NLP.

Bateson suggested that the brain, in fact any biological or social system, is organised into levels. We all operate at different levels of thinking and being. Dilts assumes five levels of operation:

The basic level of operation is our **environment**, the external constraints we work within. We operate on that environment through our **behaviour.** Our behaviour is guided by our mental maps and our strategies, which define our **capabilities.** These capabilities are organised by **belief and values** systems, and these are organised by our **identity.**

As you read this book you're interacting with the environment – your body is adjusting to temperature and your

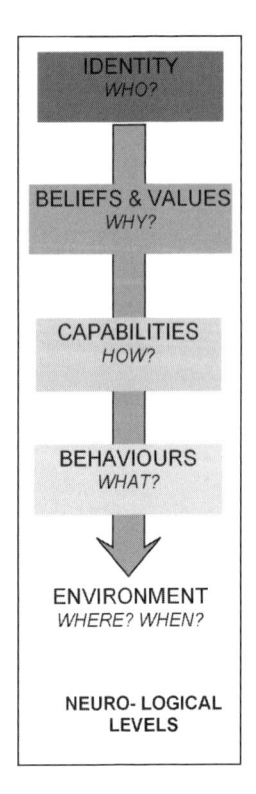

IDENTITY
WHO?

BELIEFS & VALUES
WHY?

CAPABILITIES
HOW?

BEHAVIOURS
WHAT?

ENVIRONMENT
WHERE? WHEN?

NEURO- LOGICAL LEVELS

behaviour will reflect this – if you're cold you'll shiver or go and get something warm. Once you're snug again you'll continue your previous behaviour – reading this book. The fact that you can read it demonstrates one of your capabilities. The fact that it's a book about hypnosis and therapy shows that you have a value – something you find important – about the subject. Whether it's the best thing you've ever read or you want to throw it in the bin has as much to do with your beliefs about the subject as it does the actual content. Finally – you know it's you reading the book and not someone else. Go and have a peek in the mirror if you're in any doubt. In all situations these levels are in action.

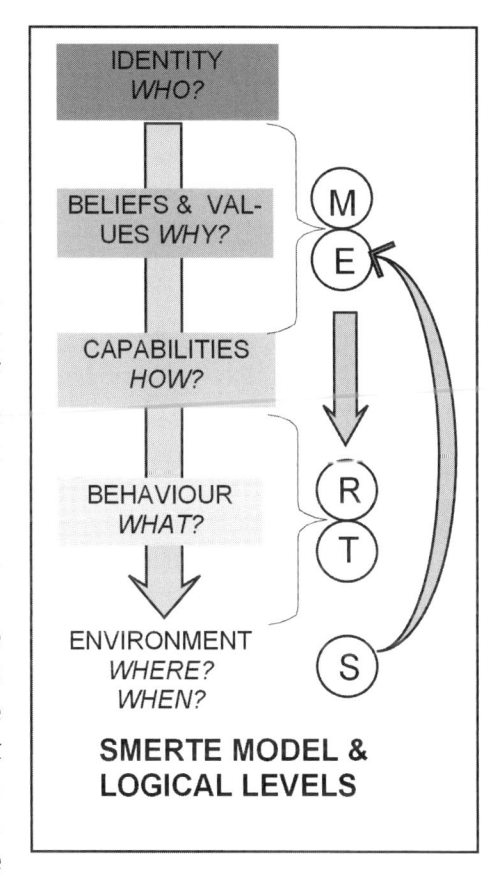

| IDENTITY WHO? |
| BELIEFS & VALUES WHY? |
| CAPABILITIES HOW? |
| BEHAVIOUR WHAT? |
| ENVIRONMENT WHERE? WHEN? |

SMERTE MODEL & LOGICAL LEVELS

M
E
R
T
S

If we link this model to Wolinsky's idea of trance identities we could say instead that each trance identity will have beliefs that define and limit them, which will generate a perception of a lack of capabilities (negative hallucination), which will produce behaviour that supports the identity (such as a person who has a belief 'I'm stupid,' who seizes up before an exam)

The environment will often be the trigger for the emergence of this trance identity, as it provides the context for the behaviour (in this case an exam room). In the graphic above you can see how this then connects with the SMERTE model you have already used:

Each trance identity a person has is generated from a memory matrix that forms in response to the emotional meaning the memories are given. These meanings are expressed as beliefs, such as 'I'm a loser,' 'I'm stupid,' 'I deserve to be punished.' In response to these beliefs we will develop values around what is important to us, and what is not. These values will motivate us to act, or not to act, as the case may be. Our capabilities in situations controlled by a trance identity are likely to be limited. As an example, I used to have a trance identity generated by DIY. The thought of doing anything practical would generate a *belief* around 'It will go wrong, it always does...' (inevitability). This gave rise to the limitations I felt I had about my practical skills (capabilities), which led to avoidance *behaviour* whenever I could get away with it. When I couldn't avoid it the post-hypnotic suggestion inherent in my belief nearly always came true.

Within NLLs each level organises the levels below it, so in therapy the higher the level you influence the more profound effect you are likely to have. The same is often true of the SMERTE model. This might be why Behaviourist approaches take so long to have an effect, they are at too low a level, and why some NLP interventions that are working at the behavioural level often only have a temporary effect.

Appendix 3

The meta-model

The meta-model derives from the modelling of Virginia Satir and Fritz Perls by Bandler and Grinder. Both were outstanding therapists who had a particular way of gathering information. They would use their questions to recover the information in people's conversation that was left unsaid. It can be enormously useful in clarifying the clients' thoughts and uncovering their automatic processes.

To understand how it works we need to look at the structure of language.

Deep structure and surface structure

Speech is such an automatic process that most of us are oblivious of the passage a thought takes from its mental inception to its physical expression.

The words we use to express our thoughts cannot contain their full meaning. To communicate in words

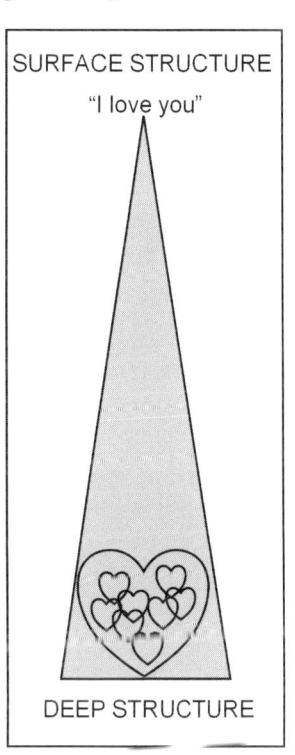

SURFACE STRUCTURE
"I love you"

DEEP STRUCTURE

what we experience in a single second of an experience, like a roller-coaster, a first kiss, or a driving test, would take much more than that second, so language is reductive.

Have you ever been in love and found that word totally insufficient for the scale of the feelings you have? That is the limitation of language. Such limitations are necessary to enable us to handle and communicate the vast amount of information potentially available to us at any one moment. Not to mention how bored we would get with people giving us the whole version of everything (which not even the most talkative of people can achieve).

Noam Chomsky, the American linguist, made a distinction between the surface structure of language, and the deep structure of language.

'I love you' represents the surface structure. All the feelings that accompany it, which may have no word equivalents, are the deep structure.

If I say, 'My friend is lazy,' I have represented something at a surface level. All other information connected to that statement (compared to who, in what way, according to whom) forms the deep structure of the surface statement. We create surface structure using the same filters on our thoughts that are applied to the information coming from our senses – deletion, distortion, and generalisation.

The meta-model organises common language patterns into these three main types. It then gives standard responses to those patterns that help to elicit the deeper meaning behind the words used.

Your purpose in using the meta-model is to:

- Recover deletions
- Correct distortions
- Expose generalisations

By doing so you will reveal to your clients any ambiguity in their thoughts, clarify any vagueness and elicit specific meaning from their model of the world. In other words you gain clarity about the way their mind creates their problem pattern.

Appendix 4

Meta-model questions

Deletions

Nominalisations are verbs that pretend to be nouns. When people use them they generally turn something that is an action into a static concept. Examples are words like education and relationship. If a client says 'I'm in a bad relationship,' they're speaking as if it's something physical that they could actually show you. The meta-model turns them back into verbs, turns them from a static state, into something with movement, which makes them much more adaptable.

> Example: I'm in a bad relationship.
> Response: How are you not relating well?
> Example: Communication around here is non-existent.
> Response: Who fails to communicate with whom? What do you want to communicate?

UNSPECIFIED VERBS

As my junior-school teacher used to make us chant, 'verbs are doing words.' Unspecified verbs are simply verbs that occur in a sentence that doesn't supply the evidence to support it – the how about the what. 'He annoyed me.'

> 'How, specifically, did he annoy you?'
> 'He hurt me.'
> 'How, specifically, did he hurt you?'

SIMPLE DELETIONS

All sentences contain simple deletions. As with presuppositions, without them our communication would be too long to be feasible. Things like, 'I'm stupid,' and 'You're wrong' are examples. The meta-model response recovers the evidence for these statements.

> 'I'm stupid.'
> 'How do you know? What is it that makes you think so?'
> 'You're wrong?'
> 'About what? How do you know? According to whom?'
> 'I'm sad. I'm fed up.'
> 'About what?'

LACK OF REFERENTIAL INDEX

I'm sure there are good academic reasons for the names of some of these classifications, but in the real world – why couldn't they have been called something simpler? Anyway, this group is words that are not supported by the evidence of what or whom they're referring to. Words like he/she, they, it and that are common examples.

> 'They don't love me.'
> 'Who, specifically, doesn't love you?'
> 'He doesn't care.'
> 'Who doesn't care?'

'He broke it'
'Who broke what?'

COMPARATIVE DELETIONS

This is where a comparison is being made, but where the thing being compared to is not specified. Words to watch for: 'good', 'better', 'more', 'less', 'most', least', 'worse', 'worst':

'He's the worst boss.'
'Compared to whom?'
'She is better than me.'
'At what, specifically?'

I once had someone ring for an appointment, who asked how much I charged. I told him and he exclaimed, 'Wow, that's expensive!' Some would defend their charges with an indignant 'No it's not!' or something puffy-chested like 'Well, I'm worth it.'

Instead I used the meta-model and asked, 'Really, compared to what?'

He thought for a while and then said 'Well, guitar lessons.'

I agreed with him, and bringing the incongruity of his comparison to the surface seemed to resolve the issue and he booked the appointment.

Distortions

MIND READING

This one at least does what it says on the tin. It's simply where the person presumes to know the thoughts of others.

'You don't like me.'
'How do you know that I don't like you?'
'He thinks I'm stupid.'
'How do you know?'

Lost performative

Where a value judgment is implied, without mention of its origin. We all have rules in our heads that we've absorbed as our own over time, and can still respond to situations using these rules as guides, even if we've outgrown them.

> 'It's wrong to criticise.'
> 'How do you know it's wrong?'
> 'He shouldn't go out without me.'
> 'Who says he shouldn't?'
> 'I can't leave her, it's not right'.
> 'According to whom?'

Cause and effect

Familiar to us from Volume I, one of the three algorithms of the mind. In this context a belief that an external factor forces a response in you. I've heard this referred to as a *cause and effect violation,* but it sounds a bit violent to me. The principle behind it is that nothing makes us do or feel anything, at some level we choose our responses to situations – but of course when we're emotionally hijacked it's usually a trance identity that does the choosing for us.

> 'You make me feel guilty.'
> 'How does what I'm doing **cause** you to feel guilty?'
> 'She makes me angry.'
> 'How does what she is doing make you angry?'

Complex equivalence

(A = B – this is the same as that.) The second of the three algorithms. Again based on connections between two or more things that don't have to be connected together, but have been by the client's unconscious calculations.

'You're always shouting at me — you don't care about me!'
'How does shouting at you mean I don't care? Have you ever shouted at someone you care about?'
'If he loved me he wouldn't work late.'
'How does him working late mean he doesn't love you?'

PRESUPPOSITIONS

Familiar territory from Volume I, the linguistic equivalent of assumptions. Refer back for the full description. In the meta-model the purpose is to listen for the presuppositions in the clients' conversation. What assumptions are they making that they might be unaware of?

'If my husband knew how tired I was, he wouldn't ask me.'
'How do you know he doesn't know?'

Generalisations

UNIVERSAL QUANTIFIERS

When people are in the grip of strong emotions they often fall into the trap of seeing the one thing they're focusing on as being representative of everything relating to it. Listen for words like *always, never, everyone, no one*.

'She never listens to me.'
'Never? What would happen if she did?'
'And all of my friends agree with me about her.'
'All of them?'
'I've never been confident about anything.'
'Never? About anything?'

Modal operators of necessity

Another example of rules operating in the background. Very often artefacts of the past. Words to watch for: *should, shouldn't, must, must not, have to, need to, it's necessary*:

> 'I have to finish this tonight.'
> 'What would happen if you didn't?'
> 'I have to stay in the marriage.'
> 'What would happen if you didn't?'

Modal operators of possibility/impossibility

Words to watch for: *can, can't, will, won't, may, may not, possible, impossible*:

> 'I will not pass this exam.'
> 'What will prevent you passing it? What would happen if you did pass?'
> 'If this goes on much longer I may lose my temper.'
> 'What would happen if you did?' 'What would happen if you didn't?'

Meta-model exercise

Respond to the following statements identifying and using the correct meta-model question. Afterwards have a partner ask you them at random to test your speed of identification. It will improve with practice.

1. 'He is the laziest man.'
2. 'He hated me.'
3. 'It is impossible to reason with her.'
4. 'Every time I make advances she turns me down.'
5. 'He must hate me, he never talks to me.'

6 'She makes me feel so inadequate.'
7 'It's wrong to be so late.'
8 'You think I'm mad.'
9 'I am stupid.'
10 'I must get back with my husband.'

Some people find it easy to remember the labels of the different patterns, others struggle. The names are not important – unless you are an NLP trainer! What is important is that you recognise the patterns, and learn to ask the right question in response.

When learning the meta-model it will help to keep this sequence in mind:

> Listen to what the person says
> Repeat it to yourself
> Ask yourself, 'What have they missed out?'

As you become more familiar with the patterns you will recognise that many sentences contain more than one, for example: 'He never pays attention to me' contains both a lack of referential index, a universal quantifier, and a nominalisation. Which would give you the most useful information? It will vary from situation to situation, but in most cases deletions are least valuable, followed by generalisations and then distortions.

At this stage it might seem impossible to think fast enough to make this choice, but with practice you'll find the pattern with the most leverage appears obvious.

Soft front ends

One of the most important things with the meta-model is to use it sparingly. Over-zealous use of it can lead to violence! (Don't ask me how specifically or it will start with you!) Elegance is a key factor in all aspects of NLP, and the meta-model is no exception. In its basic form it can sound very harsh and an easy way to break rapport (I told you not to ask how specifically, you're really winding me up!) is to use it in this way. Softening the front end can make it more covert. Commonly used soft front ends are:

> 'I just want to check what you're saying, what do you mean by...?'
> 'I'm just wondering how C causes E.'
> 'Can you imagine, just for a moment, what would happen if...?'

Try them with and without a soft front end and notice the difference.

Appendix 5

Reframing

Reframing means to put a new or different slant on some image or experience. In therapeutic terms it means to transform some portion of a client's experience by changing its meaning, or its context.

A 'frame' relates to the cognitive dimensions our mind constructs around a situation – the way in which the mind has deleted, distorted and generalised the information to give the situation its meaning. A reframe, then, becomes the means by which a therapist causes the clients to redefine the situation – by becoming aware of something deleted (or causing something new to be deleted), to distort the situation in some new way, or either to undo a generalisation that has contributed to the meaning, or create a new one.

The way a situation is framed influences the interpretation of the event. A painful moment can seem overwhelming when viewed from the perspective of a frame that comprises only seconds either side of the moment. Zooming out to view that moment from the perspective of a whole lifetime may make the moment seem trivial. 'Reframing' in this manner is one of the most powerful weapons in a therapist's armoury, and revolves around the ability to do just one thing:

Listen to anything a client says and ask yourself, 'What else could this mean, which if it did, would create a useful change in the client's model of the world?' (particularly in relation to the client's problem).

The way a photographer frames a shot is a good metaphor for reframing. Whether she chooses to use a tree as a centrepiece of the shot, or use it to frame the robin sitting on one of its branches will change the information in the picture, the balance of foreground and background, and the response to the picture by those observing it.

So the framing of an experience determines to a great degree the response to it when it is observed. Change the frame and you'll often change the response.

In NLP reframing involves shifting the focus around the content of an experience or situation, changing our perception of the situation so that it may be handled more resourcefully. NLP has identified two fundamental forms of reframing: *context* and *content* reframing.

Context reframing

According to Leslie Cameron-Bandler (1978) contextual reframing in NLP 'accepts all behaviours as useful in some context'. Rain, for example, may spell disaster for a Wimbledon crowd, but salvation for an Ethiopian farmer. The rain itself is neither 'good' nor 'bad', it is where and when it falls (context) that will attract a value judgment. The purpose of contextual reframing is to change a person's negative internal response to a particular behaviour by realising the usefulness of it in some other context. This allows us to see the behaviour as simply a behaviour (like the rain) and shift our attention to addressing the issues relating to the larger context (i.e., how can we rain-proof Wimbledon, or create an economy in Ethiopia that is not so dependent on rain?).

An example in therapy would be a client who came to see me complaining of a lack of assertiveness. In regression we went back to an incident at school when she backed down to a bully and took it to mean that she was weak. One of the things I said was, 'If there was a quality you have developed as a result of this experience that you wouldn't want to lose, what would it be?' (As in 'out of your wound...'.)

She thought for a while and replied, 'Well, actually, I am not threatening to people and so they open up to me easily, which is useful when I think of it because I'm doing a lot of workplace counselling.'

'And when you look at the action you took at the time, was it actually weakness?'

'No, it was bloody sensible, she was a monster!' She thought a little bit more and said, 'Later, we were never actually friends, but we did a project together in biology and got on okay, she had a lot of problems at home.'

'So do you think the way you were back then helped her to open up to you?'

'Yes, quite possibly.'

The behaviour that she had labelled as weakness actually becomes a strength later in her life (a different context). Once she is aware of this it is easy to reframe the meaning of the behaviour at the time it occurs as well.

Content reframing

Instead of shifting the context, the second form of reframing involves giving a different meaning to something by shifting the perspective or the intent of the viewer. Take a bamboo cane placed in a room. It is a physical object with no inherent meaning. A public-school boy walking into the room might respond to the cane in a much different way from a gardener. It is they who are supplying the meaning to the cane.

A man is enjoying a drive along a sunny country lane in his new open-topped sports car. As he approaches a corner a woman in another car comes careering round it on the wrong side of the road, forcing him to take avoiding action and nearly leaving him in a ditch. As the woman drives past he hears her shout 'Pig!' He thinks 'What a bloody nerve,' and turns and shouts back 'Bitch!' Feeling better for that he drives round the corner...and hits the pig.

Content reframing involves exploring the intention behind a person's external behaviour. In NLP this is most commonly accomplished by finding the positive intention or purpose behind a particular symptom or problematic behaviour. This is often what we seek to achieve in time-line recoding above the first event connected to the issue, by asking such questions as:

> TS: When your father shouted at you for not passing the test, what was his intention?
> C: To make me work harder.
> TS: And why did he want that?
> C: So I'd get a better job.
> TS: So did he shout at you because he didn't love you, or because he did?

By separating intention from behaviour it is much simpler to de-identify the client from the meaning he/she gave to a situation – and any decisions made about him/herself as a result.

One-word reframing exercise

A simple way to practise both content and context reframing is to explore one-word reframes of other words. This is done by taking a word expressing a particular idea or concept and finding another word for that idea or concept that puts either a more positive or negative slant on it.

As Bertrand Russell once pointed out, 'I am firm; you are obstinate; he is a pig-headed fool.'

Other examples could include:

> 'She is fat; you are plump; I am big-boned.'
> 'He is stupid; you are impetuous; I am intuitive.'

'I have reconsidered; you have changed your mind; he has gone back on his word.'

Task

Do the same for the following:

- ☐ Responsible
- ☐ Playful
- ☐ Stable
- ☐ Frugal
- ☐ Assertive

Being able to take a client's point of view and subtly shift its emphasis so he/she suddenly thinks of it in a new way is a skill that is well worth investing time in developing. Whoever said 'every cloud has a silver lining' may have been the first reframer in history.

Appendix 6

Suggestion starters

And you might wonder....

It might not be until later that you notice....

And it may not be until afterwards, looking back that you realise....

And we can both wonder when....

So if your unconscious mind could....

You might be surprised....

And we don't know yet what is to be the first thing that means....

So whether it happens now or later doesn't matter, just that....

And more quickly than you might imagine....

And the more curious you become about this the more....

And it might not be until the third or fourth time it happens that you notice for the first time that....

And whatever is the first small thing that means....

So as you continue to....

Many things can begin to....

And it could be many things that let you know you're changing....

Gradually and gently you soon....

After a while it just becomes normal that....

And whether it's you or someone else who notices first....

It might be amusing just how surprised people are when you....

Looking back you might find it easy to forget to remember....

Glossary

A

Adverb/adjective modifier
> Presupposition that modifies the meaning of another word, like **comfortable** chair.

Age regression
> Trance phenomena during which attention is focussed on a past experience.

Age progression
> Trance phenomena during which attention is focussed on a possible future experience.

Algorithms of the mind
> The three ways the mind assesses information flowing through the senses; $C>E$ (this is because of that), $A=B$ (this is the same as that), and $A=$ not B (this is different to that).

Amnesia
> Trance phenomenon that causes a block to recall of a particular piece of information.

Anchor
> Linking a stimulus to an emotional response. Anchors can be physical – applying pressure to a knuckle, but work in any modality. Linking a smell to a positive state, for example.

Asperger's Syndrome
> A milder form of autism characterised by social isolation and eccentric behaviour.

Association
> Where a person experiences a thought as if through his/her own eyes, often with the full emotional connections associated with the thought.

Awareness
> Presupposition whereby the listener's attention is directed to information from a specific sense...whatever it is you begin to hear that....

B

Behaviour
> Neuro-logical level that describes the actions we take, corresponds to the response stage of the MM.

Behaviour cycle
> Model that suggests that my attitude affects my behaviour, which affects your attitude, which affects your behaviour, which affects....

Beliefs
> Neuro-logical level. Things we take to be true that order our model of the world.

Bind
> Milton model pattern where the listener is moved to make a choice between two therapeutically useful things, or where the acceptance of one thing is accepted as inevitably leading to something else.

Butterfly effect
> Originally identified by the meteorologist Edward Lorenz, this phenomenon was popularised by the analogy that a butterfly flapping its wings in the Amazon could result in a thunderstorm in Australia – hence the 'butterfly effect'. Its technical name is 'sensitive dependence on initial conditions'. It affects any complex, dynamic system. In

Cognitive Hypnotherapy it is assumed that the mind is such a system.

C

Calculations
> Term used in Cognitive Hypnotherapy to describe the action of the brain when contemplating possibilities based on previously stored meanings.

Capabilities
> Neuro-logical level that describes a person's strengths, resources, abilities.

Cause and effect
> The concept that an action or event will produce a certain response to the action in the form of another event. Present in Cognitive Hypnotherapy as one of the algorithms of the mind, and in NLP as part of the meta and Milton models.

Change-link pattern
> A Wordweaving™ pattern that uses the clients' evidence of improvement in their experience to create an anticipation of its continuation.

Cognitive Hypnotherapy
> A therapeutic approach that combines ideas drawn from cognitive theory, evolutionary psychology, NLP, positive psychology, and uses a theory of trance states proposed by Steven Wolinsky within the approach to suggestion developed by Trevor Silvester (Wordweaving™) to create a brief therapy model.

Cognitive theory
> Concerns itself with how we form our perceptions – how we come to know. Has at its heart the idea that we are all scientists devising and testing theories about how the world works.

Complex equivalence
> Used in Cognitive Hypnotherapy to describe one of the three algorithms of the mind (A = B). Where one thing is

taken to be the same as, or have the same qualities as, another. In NLP one of the Milton and meta-model patterns.

Consequence
> One of the four categories that form a client's problem pattern; the hallucination of the future imagined as a result of a present situation, itself based on past experiences that are deemed similar.

Context
> One of the four categories that form a problem pattern; the circumstances within which a problem occurs (or doesn't) and the history behind its formation.

Context mapping
> The process of questioning that establishes and defines the boundaries of the presenting issue – when it happens, when it doesn't, when it's worse etc.

D

Deep structure
> Originally postulated by Noam Chomsky in generative grammar, an abstract underlying structure from which the actual form of a word or sentence is derived.

Deletions
> One of Bandler and Grinder's universal modelling processes – how the mind filters information flowing through the senses and refines it from 2,000,000 bits of information down to 7 plus or minus 2. Deletion refers to the removal by the unconscious of information from conscious awareness.

Distortions
> One of Bandler and Grinder's universal modelling processes – how the mind interprets information flowing through the senses to make it what it expects to be. Why we mistake strangers walking down the street for friends.

Drivers
: Those SMDs that are the key to the meaning given to an internal representation. The difference that makes a difference.

Dissociation
: A trance phenomenon where our subjective experience is that of observing, either something we're doing, or something we're thinking. A detached, unemotional state.

D-mode thinking
: Description given by Guy Claxton for left-brain, deliberate thinking (hence the D).

E

Eden Project
: Fabulous biospheres in Cornwall, England (you know the Americans and geography) that replicate the different environments on the planet. A great day out.

Emotion
: A mental state that arises spontaneously rather than through conscious effort and is often accompanied by physiological changes. The third stage of the MM, it being emotion that drives us to act.

Emotional tuning metaprograms
: Three ways of filtering emotional information between people; sending, receiving and responding.

Environment
: Our surroundings. Within Cognitive Hypnotherapy's interpretation of NLLs, everything that is not mental (i.e. includes the body).

Evaluation
: Last step of the MM process. The mind compares the result of the process it's just run against the purpose it was originally designed for.

Evolutionary psychology
: The study of the psychological adaptations of humans to

the changing physical and social environment, especially of changes in brain structure, cognitive mechanisms, and behavioural differences among individuals.

Exception elicitation
> Part of context mapping, where the questions seek to define the extent of the problem by gaining clarity about when it doesn't happen.

G

Generalisations
> One of Bandler and Grinder's universal modelling processes – where we take an experience and use it to represent the entire category of which the experience is an example. Closely involved in belief creation and predicting consequence.

Guiding state
> A state that is post-hypnotically suggested for the client to experience at a moment when he/she would normally have a negative experience. Posited on the idea that we can't experience opposite emotions simultaneously, the client may be triggered to feel surprised/amused/curious when he/she would expect to feel anxious/scared/nervous. This interrupt disrupts the problem pattern.

I

Ideo-motor signal
> Non-verbal means of unconscious communication. Often a finger signal can be utilised through a pendulum, or the shake/nod of the head.

Identity
> One of the NLLs. Identity comprises those factors from which the sense of self emerge. Includes representational system preferences, metaprograms. Identity is that person you know isn't someone else.

Internal representation
: Full term would probably be...of our external sensing. The version of reality we are aware of in our thoughts, either a memory, or the filtered information from our senses of the world outside.

L

Lack of referential index
: Language pattern from the Milton and meta-models. Where we don't identify what we're referring to directly in the sentence. 'He broke it' is an example. Who's he and what's it?

M

Matrix model (MM)
: A model used in Cognitive Hypnotherapy to describe the steps the mind and body make from the awareness of a stimulus to the conclusion of its response to it. The sequence it describes is stimulus-memory matrix-emotion-response-termination-evaluation.

Memory matrix
: A chain of memories connected by a particular context – from the first reference experience, usually a significant emotional event, to the present day. The second step of the MM.

Meta-model
: NLP question model that seeks to bring to awareness distortions, deletions and generalisations that derive from a client's deep structure and form part of the client's model of the world.

Meta programs
: A series of filters that organise information and guide and direct other mental processes.

Milton Model
    A set of language patterns modelled by Bandler and Grinder from the hypnotic language of Milton Erickson.

Modal operator
    A Milton and meta-model category characterised by words like 'can', 'may', 'might' (possibility) and 'must', 'should', 'can't' (necessity).

N

Negative hallucination
    Trance phenomenon whereby the person doesn't notice something that is in view.

Neuro-linguistic programming
    Defined as 'the study of subjective experience' and originally developed by Bandler and Grinder, it has grown to include a number of models that are useful in developing excellence in a wide range of human activities.

Neuro-logical Levels (NLLs)
    Developed by Robert Dilts who was inspired by Gregory Bateson's work on classifying natural hierarchies. Dilts applied these ideas to the nervous system and proposed that different logical levels are an expression of different types of neurological organisation that operate at different levels.

Neuron
    A brain cell.

O

Occam's razor
    Occam's (or Ockham's) razor is a principle attributed to the fourteenth-century logician and Franciscan friar, William of Occam. Ockham was the village in the English county of Surrey where he was born. The modern version of it states 'when you have two competing theories that make

exactly the same predictions, the one that is simpler is the better.' Echoed by Bruce Lee when he said: 'True refinement seeks simplicity.'

Ordinal
: A presuppositional language pattern that revolves around the use of a number ('the first thing you may notice').

Orr's Law
: Imagine the mind has two elements, the thinker and the prover. 'What the thinker thinks the prover proves.'

Outcome
: The end point of therapy – the client's solution state.

P

Pattern hunting
: Term used in Cognitive Hypnotherapy to describe the purpose of the therapist when listening to a client. A problem comprises a pattern made of context, structure, process and consequence. The therapist's task is to hunt for this pattern within the information clients provides about their issue.

Pleasure principle
: Freudian idea (that still holds true). We are motivated to move towards pleasure and away from pain. The primary reflex of the unconscious.

Positive hallucination
: Trance phenomenon whereby we see something that isn't there, or we interpret visual information in a particular way that may not be objectively true, i.e. looking at an audience and seeing interested faces.

Possibility
: See Modal operator.

Premature evaluation
: Where the immature mind draws conclusions from its limited understanding of the world. These conclusions often drive problematic behaviour in adulthood and are

the target of techniques aimed at reframing the beliefs that arise from them.

Presuppositions
The linguistic equivalent of assumptions. Things in a sentence we tend to accept unconsciously as true in order to make sense of that sentence.

Priming
Priming is an acuteness to stimuli because of exposure to a certain event or experience. For example, an individual who has just purchased a new car may now start to notice with more frequency other people driving her same make and model. This person has been primed to recognise more readily a car like hers because of the experience she has driving and owning one.

Problem state
The total experience of the client in the context of his issue.

Process
One of the four categories of information that comprise a problem pattern. Process describes the 'doing' of the client's problem as it occurs. Process is what the MM describes.

Prover
See Orr's Law.

R

Receivers
One part of the emotional tuning metaprograms. Describes an individual's receptivity to emotional information being communicated by another.

Recoding
The act of changing mental programming so that a thought is stored and experienced in a different way.

Reference experience
An experience that is significant enough to an individual

to become something used by the mind to measure the meaning of subsequent events.

Reframing
: Taking a piece of information and changing the meaning of it by offering a new perspective.

Representational system
: From NLP. The sense that a person is representing the world through at any particular moment. NLP postulates that most people have a preference for which sense they pay most attention to, and that this has a big impact on how he/she interacts with the world.

Responders
: One part of the emotional tuning metaprograms. Describes an individual's tendency to respond to emotional information being communicated by another as if it's his own.

Response
: Part of the MM, describes the behaviour created by the unconscious in response to a particular stimulus.

S

Selection restriction violation
: Language pattern from the Milton and meta-models. Describes when we attribute animate characteristics to objects, e.g. 'the chair was comforting.'

Senders
: One part of the emotional tuning metaprograms. Describes an individual's ability to send emotional information to another, and to infect her with it.

Sensory distortion
: Trance phenomenon where information from a sense other than visual is changed into something other than how it would normally be perceived, e.g. getting chocolate to taste of lard.

Significant Emotional Event (SEE)
: An event that the unconscious takes to be important as a

reference experience in relation to emotions such as anger, fear, sadness guilt, not being loved, etc.

Solution state
The point of therapy. The evidence by which the client would know that he/she no longer has the problem.

Stimulus
Starting point of the MM. The situation, person or object that is matched by the unconscious, using the three algorithms of the mind, to something from the past, which causes a response to be generated.

Structure
Trance phenomena and sub-modalities are of the four categories of information that comprise a problem pattern. Structure is about how we subjectively experience a thought. Sub-modalities are usually the means to describe the structure of a problem pattern.

Sub-modalities (SMDs)
The building blocks of meaning. Where the five senses can be described as modalities, SMDs describe the qualities that make up our perception of a thought, such as whether we think of it in black and white or colour. NLP suggests some SMDs are key to the meaning we give to the thought. These are known as drivers.

Suggestion loop
A single unit of a wordweaving pattern or script that incorporates at least one suggestion from each of the NLLs, using C>E or complex equivalence to connect the lower three to a new belief, value or sense of identity.

Surface structure
The words we use to describe the abstract underlying (deep) structure from which the actual form of a sentence is derived. From this concept comes the idea that words are not the thing they represent. Korzypski: 'The map is not the territory.'

T

Termination
: From the MM. The point at which the response to the stimulus ceases.

Thinker
: See Orr's Law.

Time
: Presuppositional use of words that focus attention on our experience of the passing of time.

Time distortion
: Trance phenomenon whereby our subjective experience of time is altered, i.e. an awareness of it passing quickly or slowly.

Terror management theory (TMT)
: The theory that we cope with our fear of death by connecting to, and defending, things that will live beyond us, like culture or family. Our life might just be a distraction from our scariest thought.

Trance phenomena
: An everyday part of our mental processes through which our model of the world is created and perceived. Utilised deliberately in Cognitive Hypnotherapy to guide the client to a more positive perception.

U

Universal modelling processes
: Bandler and Grinder's model of how the mind reduces the 2,000,000 bits of information flowing through its senses each moment, down to roughly 7 plus or minus 2, and by doing so creates a model of reality that we mistake for the whole thing. The processes are deletion, distortion and generalisation.

V

Values
> Part of the NLLs. Values are the things we use to gauge the importance of things. They motivate us to act, and offer a means of evaluation.

Bibliography

The Adapted Mind by Barkow, Cosmides and Tooby, OUP, 1992.
The Age of Spiritual Machines by Ray Kurzweil, Penguin (USA), 2000.
Authentic Happiness by Martin Seligman, Nicholas Brealey Publishing, 2003.
Beyond Words: Languaging Change Through the Quantum Field by John Overdorf and Julie Silverthorn, audiotape, 1995.
The Denial of Death by Ernest Becker, Simon & Schuster, 1997.
Did You Spot the Gorilla?: How to Recognise the Hidden Opportunities in Your Life by Professor Richard Wiseman, Arrow, 2004.
Emergence by Steven Johnson, Penguin, 2001.
Emotional Contagion by Hatfield, Cacioppo and Rapson, CUP, 1994
Emotions Revealed by Paul Ekman, Weidenfeld & Nicolson, 2003.
Hare Brain Tortoise Mind by Guy Claxton, Fourth Estate Ltd, 1998.
Hypnotic Language by John Burton and Bob G. Bodenhamer, Crown House, 2000.
'Imaging studies show how brain thinks about pain' by Constance Holden, *Science*, vol 303.

Introducing Evolutionary Psychology by Dylan Evans and Oscar Zarate, Icon Books, 1999.
Iron John by Robert Bly, Element (USA), 1992.
The Luck Factor by Professor Richard Wiseman, Arrow, 2004.
In Search of Solutions by William Hudson O'Hanlon and Michelle Weiner-Davis, W. W. Norton (USA), 1989.
Mind Wide Open by Steven Johnson, Penguin Books Ltd, 2005.
NLP Encyclopedia by Robert Dilts, http://www.nlpuniversitypress.com.
NLP Practitioner Manual by Tad James, 1992.
The Origin of Consciousness in the Breakdown of the Bicameral Mind by Julian Jaynes, Penguin Books Ltd, 1993.
Solutions by Leslie Cameron-Bandler, Real People Press, 1985.
The Structure of Magic by Bandler and Grinder, Science and Behavior Books (USA), 1975.
The Wisdom of Milton H. Erickson by Ronald A. Havens, Crown House, 2003.

Notes

1. William Hudson O'Hanlon, Michelle Weiner-Davis, *In Search of Solutions*, W. W. Norton (USA), 1989, p52.
2. Ray Kurzweil, *The Age of Spiritual Machines*, Penguin (USA), 2000, p77.
3. Ibid.
4. Tad James, *NLP Practitioner Manual*, 1992.
5. John Overdorf, Julie Silverthorn, *Beyond Words: Languaging Change Through the Quantum Field* (audiotape), 1995.
6. Ronald A. Havens, *The Wisdom of Milton H. Erickson*, Crown House, 2003, p171.
7. Robert Dilts, *NLP Encyclopedia*, http://www.nlpuniversitypress.com.
8. Constance Holden, 'Imaging studies show how brain thinks about pain', *Science*, vol 303, p1157.
9. University of Colorado ezine, http://web.uccs.edu/ur/communique/ezine/features/04_10_02F2.htm.
10. Ibid.
11. Professor Richard Wiseman, *Did You Spot the Gorilla?: How to Recognise the Hidden Opportunities in Your Life*, Arrow, 2004, p45.
12. Professor Richard Wiseman, *The Luck Factor*, Arrow, 2004, p37.

13 Robert Bly, *Iron John*, Element (USA), 1992, p42.
14 Bandler and Grinder, *The Structure of Magic*, Preface, Science and Behavior Books (USA), 1975, pviii.
15 Guy Claxton, *Hare Brain Tortoise Mind*, Fourth Estate Ltd, 1998, p50.
16 Dylan Evans, Oscar Zarate, *Introducing Evolutionary Psychology*, Icon Books, 1999, p8.
17 John Burton, Bob G. Bodenhamer, *Hypnotic Language*, Crown House, 2000, p117.

Index

A

A = B (see complex equivalence)
Adverb/adjective modifier   47, 53,
Age Regression/Progression   67, 70, 79, 84, 113, 123, 131
Algorithms of the mind   62, 65, 154, 156
Anterior Insula   89
Anterior Cingulate Cortex   89
Artificial Intelligence   15
Aspergers syndrome   88
Attainable Outcomes   35
Audio/tory   26, 80, 123

B

Bandler, Richard   27, 79, 154, 162, 175
Bateson, Gregory   38, 172
Becker, Ernest   116
Beckham, David   136
Behaviour (NLL)   95, 138
Behaviour Cycle   130
Behaviourist   11
Beliefs (NLL)   96, 129
Bind   53
Bly, Robert   131
Boltzman, Ludwig   134
Boyne, Gil   60, 78, 104,
Boynian Pattern   ix, 63, 64, 73, 77, 123
Bragg, Lawrence   163
Butterfly Effect   20

C

Cacioppo, John   86
Calibrate   110
Cameron-Bandler, Leslie   187
Capabilities (NLL)   95, 133
Cause and Effect   17, 48, 55, 56, 57, 64, 67, 77, 96, 181
Change-Link Pattern   73, 106, 110, 121, 140, 150
Chomsky, Noam   176
Churchill, Winston   124
Claxton, Guy   135
Cognitive Hypnotherapy   11, 13, 16, 27, 58, 81, 85, 152, 153-163
Cognitive Psychology   155, 157
Cognitive Theory   14
Complex Equivalence   48, 53, 56, 57, 66, 67, 72, 77, 96, 181
Consequence   13, 49, 91, 158
Context   13, 17, 91, 158
Context mapping   18

D

Deep Structure 50, 175
Deep Trance Phenomena 82
Deletion 79, 154, 176
Deletion, Simple 179
Deletion, Comparative 180
Denial of Death 116
D-mode (deliberation) 135
Dijksterhuis 118
Dilts Robert 38, 87, 128, 172
Distortion 154, 176, 180
Drivers 25, 33

E

Ecology 42
Edison, Thomas 163
Ekman, Paul 91
Elman, Dave x, 78
Emerson, Ralph Waldo 124
Emotional Contagion 86
Emotional Hijacking 68
Emotions Revealed 91
Environment (NLL) 95, 142
Erickson, Milton 78, 133, 136, 141, 162
Ericksonian 58
Evans, Dylan 156
Evidence Procedure 34
Evolutionary Psychology 65, 157
Exception mapping 19

F

Fight/Flight Response 68
Freud, Sigmund 3, 68

G

Generalisation 81, 154, 176
Genius 136
Greenberg, Jeff 116-118
Grinder, John 79, 154, 175
Guiding State 52
Gustatory 123

Gustatory Distortion 80

H

Hare Brain Tortoise Mind 135
Hatfield, Elaine 86
Helen 5, 10, 21, 27, 30, 33, 35, 40, 67, 68, 70, 72, 73, 83, 85, 94, 97, 100, 104, 150,
Hodgkin, Jane 3
Hogan, Kevin 46
Hudson, O'Hanlon William 10
Hypnotherapy Journal ix, 62

I

Identity (NLL) 96, 128
Ideo-motor Signal 121,
Immune System 13
Internal Representation 24
Iron John 131

J

Jaynes, Julian 135
Jungian 11
James, Tad 48, 90

K

Kinaesthetic 26, 29, 36, 123
Kurzweil, Ray 14, 15, 124

L

Lack of Referential Index 179
Lost performative 181
Lubbock, John 124
Luck Factor The 125

M

Matrix Model 30, 32
Maxwell, James Clark 134, 136
Mental Modules 158
Meta Model 16, 79, 175-185
Metaprograms 91
Milton Model 79
Mind reading 180
Modelling 63

Model Operator of Necessity 49, 183
Model Operator of Possibility 52, 54, 55, 56, 183

N

Negative Hallucination 79, 84
Neurons 14
Neuro-Linguistic Programming (NLP) ix, 16, 25, 37, 49, 50, 62, 63, 81, 86, 91, 133, 142
Neuro-logical Levels 30, 32, 37, 53, 65, 128, 143, 172-174
Nominalisations 178
Nominal Processing 159, 167

O

Occam's Razor 62
Oedipus Complex 11
Olfactory 123
Ordinal (Presupposition)
Origin of Consciousness in the Breakdown of the Bicameral Mind, The 135
Orr's Law 49, 66, 80, 114, 153, 167
Overdorf, John 65

P

Pattern Hunting/Recognition 13, 14, 124
Perls, Fritz x, 104, 157, 175
Perot, Ross 142
Piaget 159, 167
Pleasure Principle, The 68, 154
Poincare 133
Post Hypnotic Suggestion 81, 101,
Positive Hallucination 67, 80, 84, 105,
Positive Psychology 114
Pragmatism 150
Presuppositions 46, 182
Presupposition of Awareness 52
Priming 123, 126, 140, 142,150

Problem Focussed 11
Problem Pattern 17, 30, 58, 82, 109, 110, 159
Problem State 12, 13, 44, 110,
Process 13, 51, 91, 158
Prover/Thinker 49, 153, 158, 167
Psychanalyst 11
Pyke, Penny 139
Pyszczynski, Tom 115, 116-118

R

Rapport 16, 86, 91, 110,
Rapson, Richard 86
Realism 150
Receivers 87
Reframing 17, 110, 133, 186-190
Regression 11, 17,
Resistance 110
Responders 87
Rocking Chair Exercise 120, 132
Run on Sentence 55
Russell Bertrand 189

S

Satir, Virginia 175
Senders 86
Sensory Distortion 80, 84
Singer, Tania 89
Significant Emotional Event (SEE) 32, 67, 69, 159, 169
Silverthorn, Julie 65
Simons, Daniel 124
Socrates 136
Soloman, Sheldon 116-118
Solution Focussed 11
Solution State 12, 33, 44, 71, 83, 110, 153, 159
Splitting 58
Structure 13, 24, 27, 51, 91, 158
Submodalities (SMDs) 25, 57, 58
Suggestion loop 100

Suggestion pattern 5, 45, 77, 94, 108,
Surface Structure 50, 175
Squaw Peak 140

T

Terror Management Theory 116-118
Therapeutic Paradox 32, 116, 139, 166-171
Therapeutic Relationship 1
Thinker/Prover 49, 153, 158, 167
Time Distortion 55, 80
Trance induction 110
Trance Phenomena 53, 67, 79, 81, 83, 97, 105, 131, 154, 157, 159
Trance state 68
Transforming Therapy 60
Turing, Alan 156

U

Universal Modelling Process 79, 81, 154
Universal quantifier 182
Unspecified verbs 178

V

Values (NLL) 96, 129
Visual 26, 123
von Stradonitz 135

W

Weiner-Davis, Michelle 10
Wiseman, Richard 125, 127, 133, 138, 142
Wolinsky, Steven 67, 81, 156, 173
Wordweaving 1, 45, 56, 58, 61, 73, 82, 144, 150, 152, 159
   Three Steps of... 1, 52, 95, 97, 99

Z

Zarate, Oscar 156

Wordweaving™

The Science of Suggestion

To assist people in honing their use of hypnotic language we provide a range of further learning aids, including a card game, and an audio CD. To discover more please access our website:

www.questinstitute.co.uk

or contact our office:

The Quest Institute
Old Ness farm
Ness Road
Burwell
Cambs
CB25 0DB

Telephone 01638 720020

Wordweaving™ is a registered trademark, all rights reserved

Notes

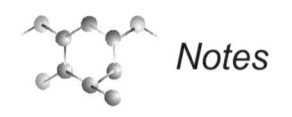

Notes

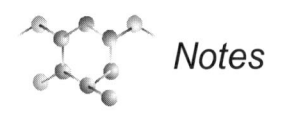

Notes

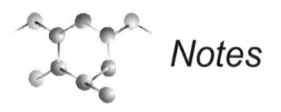

Notes

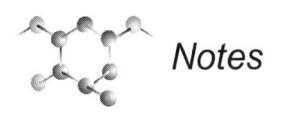

Notes

Notes

Notes

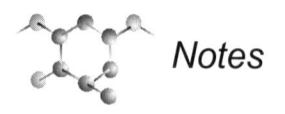

Notes

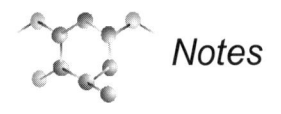

Notes

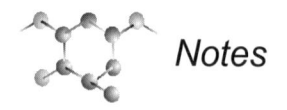

Notes

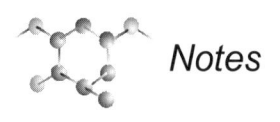

Notes

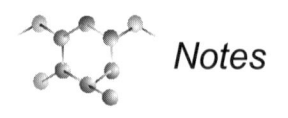

Notes

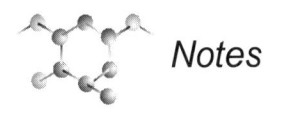

Notes